AMERICAN INJUSTICE

AMERICAN INJUSTICE

LEAVING THE PLANTATION MINDSET

DR. JOHN "JAY" HALL

Copyright © 2024 by Dr. John "Jay" Hall

All rights reserved. No part of this book may be reproduced or transmitted in any form or by any means, electronic or mechanical, including photocopying, recording or storing information in a retrieval system, without prior written permission from the publisher.

Interior Design: Creative Publishing Book Design

Printed in the United States of America

TABLE OF CONTENT

Foreword		vii
Introduction		1
Chapter One:	Letter of New U.S. Attorney Alamdar S. Hamdani	5
Chapter Two:	Hall V. City of Houston Panel Ruling	9
Chapter Three:	Fraud On the Court By Judge Lynn Hughes Case No. 4:20-Cv-03740	13
Chapter Four:	A New Lawsuit - Same Stigma Plus Narrative	27
Chapter Five:	The Exception to Res Judicata Is Fraud	31
Chapter Six:	The Failure to Investigate Under the Public And Judicial Code of Silence	33
Chapter Seven:	Breaking the Code of Silence	37
Chapter Eight:	Conclusion	47
Epilogue		57
Evidences		67

FOREWORD

The book entitled American Injustice: The Houston Code of Silence and subtitled Leaving the Plantation Mindset. It is this author's journey to fit into a southern culture which has been programmed to emasculate strong black men and women while articulating freedom but using law enforcement to suppress those freedoms. In my story, I describe how I prepared myself for roles of leadership in policing; but was derailed by jealousy, racism, and the police code of silence. In this book, I describe how my rights to life, liberty, and property were interfered with because members of law enforcement wanted my loyalty to them rather than the public that I served.

As a law enforcement professional, who was trained to be impartial and to be fair to all people, the actions taken by the individuals in this story contradicted my beliefs about justice and how people should be treated. When the actions of those who are responsible for upholding the law become corrupted, there is a need to petition the government to ensure accountability so those injustices don't become the norm and undermine our democracy.

This book presents evidence that supports my claim that our failure to address corruption of any kind by our elected officials will result in us being complicit in our own demise when we elevate people over due process of law. As a public servant and citizen, the author believes that the public needs to know when the government is not running properly. Because I chose to inform and complain about injustices in the workplace, I was subjected to a defamation of character smear campaign for 30 years. We all have heard about using law enforcement as a weapon; my story proves it. In describing his story, the author takes a dialectic approach to examine contradictions in cultures, institutions, laws, and procedures based on [race], education, and region to show the miscarriages of justice that replicate a plantation mindset in some police and judicial institutions.

This book is dedicated to my son, Martice Hall, my dad, Curtis "Red" Hall, my brothers, my cousins, who also served in the military, and Coco......... my best friend forever and my outstanding daughter, Jonquia.

INTRODUCTION

Leaving the plantation mindset is a metaphor summarizing the need for blacks to change institutions that are driven by "false narratives" and by "double standards" that are carryovers from slavery. Those false narratives suggest that blacks are at fault when we view the disproportionate quality of life indexes from a deficit model perspective rather than the systems model perspective. The deficit model finds flaws in the individual whereas the system model finds the flaws in the institutions.

Under the deficit model, the institutional gatekeepers continue to prophesize "fairness, integrity, trust, transparency, and truth seeking"; yet, the application of the rules and the allocation of resources more often than not don't align with those views. One reason for this lack of integrity is what is referred to as the code of silence. In most organizations there is a code of silence or for some a conspiracy to remain silent. When my wife was cheating on me or when I was cheating on my wife, everyone knew about the cheating but no friends would tell either one of us. My point is that we all have secrets in our private lives but how do we address secrets and or conspiracies against us in the workplace? The code of silence in the workplace covers up conspiracies and misconduct in the workplace by suppressing critical information needed to avert the harm or the employment trap that may be set for you.

This book represents my interaction with the police and the courts as a black man who chose the profession of policing but became a suspect within his own department when he blew the whistle on corruption (four millions dollars stolen without an internal affairs investigation and the manipulation of an affirmative action promotional list by political cronies).

American Injustice is not new but a reminder that institutional racism, racist gatekeepers, and Uncle Toms still promote the false narratives that we live in a color blind society. A narrative that contradicts the empirical data which shows that "gatekeepers" are still making decisions based on race rather than merit, fairness, or the law. In a profession where police officers commit suicide more often than being killed in the line of duty, I can thank the [Lord] for preserving my sanity to tell my story. However, my struggles mean nothing if others can't learn from it and use their learning to [change] it.

Dr. John "Jay" Hall is one of nine children who continues to overcome his circumstances in order to teach and to inform [his Christian sisters and brothers], lessons that will enable them to recognize [those] who wish to keep them oppressed by such programming as "look the other way" while I lie and steal from you. This book is my narrative; a narrative supported by facts and exonerating evidence; which was deliberately excluded by the gatekeepers in order

INTRODUCTION

to frame me of a [criminal offense] for twenty nine years without ever notifying me of the complaint against me and by placing complaints in my internal affairs file without notifying me. My only offense was that I refused the [three-fifth of a man standard] that the constitution initially prescribed. As you embark on the author's journey, Desmond Tutu reminds us: If you are [neutral] in situations of injustice, you have chosen the side of the oppressor. The story provides you with enough evidence that you will not remain [neutral] unless you recently received a lobotomy.

I retired from the Houston Police Department in 2004 based on HPD's refusal to allow me to transfer out of the Jail Division or acquire training from the FBI Academy due to the 1994 IAD investigation. When I retired, I retired in good standing. From 2004 to present day, I applied for over 100 law enforcement police chief jobs but was denied. In 2016, I applied for the Chief of Police position when Slyvester Turner became Mayor. I wrote him a letter indicating that I sought a name clearing hearing because I had received numerous employment denials so I believed that internal affairs had placed something in my employment files. On May 31, 2018, the new police chief, Art Acevedo, provided me with an explanation letter stating that I had been investigated in a criminal matter using wiretaps and pen registers and that the evidence was sealed by a court of law. See reference to this letter in the Chapter referenced Evidences.

Chapter One of my story starts with a letter to the U.S. Attorney's Office describing judicial corruption associated with the two lawsuits that I filed: 1) one associated with the May 31, 2018 city document and 2) the lawsuit filed when I was informed that my HPD payroll was flagged with derogatory information in October of 2022. Chapter

Two describes how the Fifth Circuit approved the dismissal of my first lawsuit without reviewing any evidence in the court record. Both the Fifth Circuit and the Federal Judge used the fabricated May 31, 2018 government record which was provided to me by Chief Arcevedo and Police Attorney Kristie Lewis. Chapter Three describes the unlawful steps taken by Judge Lynn Hughes to dismantle my civil rights lawsuit against the City of Houston. Chapter Four describes the modus operandi used by the internal affairs division to smear my reputation which consisted of flagging my payroll with untruthful information. Chapter Five describes how the City of Houston attempted to use the Res Judicata legal strategy to make my claims of discrimination and retaliation go away. Chapter Six explains how the police department, the City of Houston, and the Court used a culture of corruption which deviated from normal protocols to conceal and to destroy incriminating evidence to minimize or nullify municipal liability. Chapter Seven addresses the need for spiritual intervention to break a police culture based on the code of silence. The Conclusion and the Epilog chapters attributes the ongoing negative spiral of police misconduct to poor leadership and the failure to hold public servants accountable when complicit. And finally, the last chapter titled Evidences affords the reader an opportunity to examine city records for themselves.

CHAPTER ONE

LETTER TO THE NEW U.S. ATTORNEY ALAMDAR S. HAMDANI

In December of 2022, President Joe Biden appointed a new U.S. Attorney General. The significance of this appointment is that the new U.S. Attorney General is a Democrat and he was replacing a Republican U.S. Attorney General [Lowery]. The gatekeepers have convinced us that justice is blind and therefore, it should not matter whether a Democrat or a Republican decides a case. Unfortunately, this is not truth. My rights were denied by the very institutions that I sought justice from. On December 12, 2023, I wrote a letter to U.S. Attorney Hamdani to complain about numerous civil right violations. See first page of letter in Evidence chapter.

This complaint involves officers of the court in the form of attorneys, who were representing the City of Houston, the same Federal Judge, involved in the City of Houston affirmative action lawsuit in 1994, who refused to recuse himself, and a panel of Republican Fifth Circuit Judges, who ignored the preponderance of facts, evidence, and laws both criminally and civilly which supported appellant's civil rights claims. These individuals knowingly engaged in a conspiracy to obstruct justice.

For the record, this story is a continuation of other cases where I was framed by the internal affairs division from 2002 through 2008 for mortgage fraud by a confidential HPD informant, named Tony J. Blacknall. At that time, I was interviewed by FBI agent, Raymond Jackson regarding the Mortgage Fraud case committed by Tony J. Blacknall. After this case was over, I was contacted by a retired veteran officer, who informed me that officers in (Major Offenders Division) used Blacknall to fraudulently purchase a property using my property information without my knowledge. At the time that this happened, the police department was promoting 11 assistant chiefs. Because my name was associated with the mortgage fraud case, I was not selected but Lt. Dirden was. The retired Major Offenders officer stated that I was framed in retaliation for exposing the affirmative action promotion manipulation scheme and for exposing the four million dollars stolen from the Jail Budget without an IAD investigation.

On July 17, 2003, I complained to FBI agent, Raymond Jackson's supervisor, Russell Robinson, regarding agent Jackson's part in a conspiracy involving Michael Dirden, the lieutenant who became an Assistant Chief, with the Houston Police Department. This was the same Michael Dirden (Legal Department) who placed tainted documents in my internal affairs file without my knowledge for twenty nine years before it was revealed to me when I was told that my payroll was flagged with negative information on Oct 3, 2022 as I was requesting a new police department identification card.

Once the mortgage company contacted me regarding the fraudulent property that was purchased by Confidential Informant Tony Blacknall, I conducted my own investigation of Tony Blacknall and referred the investigation to the FBI in 2002. It took agent Jackson, five years to arrest Tony J. Blacknall. When I requested open records on this case from the police open records section, they denied having any records on this federal case. In retrospect, I figured out that the investigative divisions (Major Offenders/ Internal Affairs/ Criminal Intelligence) of the Houston Police Department were acting in retaliation by placing tainted investigations in my records by using 3 by 5 index cards to record complaints without notifying me.

As the above example suggests, the police department used their resources to conduct numerous criminal investigations which were placed in my file without my knowledge. These acts were violations of the Police Officer's **Bill** of Rights. These retaliatory actions continued for 29 years. Any time that I provided proof of police misconduct, there was no investigation conducted.

CHAPTER TWO

HALL V. CITY OF HOUSTON PANEL RULING

On August 1, 2022, I discovered that Judge Hughes and the Fifth Circuit had affirmed a legal opinion that was based on fraud. I claimed that the ruling contradicted the evidence contained in the court record. Prior to the ruling, I filed an original brief and a reply brief. I also filed a motion to have an en banc hearing which was denied. I claimed that the panel ignored the legal briefs, the facts, the evidence, and the court record excerpt containing improper motions in violation of procedural rules. Based on the panel's deliberate failure to examine the court records, I claimed that the Panel engaged in acts that were politically and racially motivated rather than based on facts and evidence contained in court records, court transcripts, pleadings, motions, and exhibits.

In the next chapter, I provide facts and evidence to contradict the Fifth Circuit Panel's published opinion. Based on these false statements, I show beyond a shadow of doubt that the published document by the Fifth Circuit Panel was an effort to cover up the fabricated May 31, 2018 government record submitted by the City of Houston. This document was cited by the FBI as fabricated.... So how is it possible that three Fifth Circuit Appeal Judges would affirm a legal opinion based on fraud. I claimed that these Judges obstructed justice. As a law enforcement practitioner, I viewed this document as a violation of the Texas Penal Code 37.09 and 37.10 and a procedural violation of Article 38.23 of the Texas Code of Criminal Procedure.

Another red flag regarding the May 31, 2018 letter, was that it referenced a criminal investigation using wiretaps and pen registers. Based on these allegations, I sought the court order authorizing both wiretaps and pen registers which should have been filed with the court as a public record. After exercising due diligence, I found no court records authorizing any wiretaps or pen registers. When I asked the City of Houston attorney to produce these records, Judge Hughes intervened and requested an in camera hearing which was a tactic to cover up the police department's illegal criminal investigation which he knew of based on ex parte communications with the City Attorney.

In addition to the criminal offenses that the Fifth Circuit panel should have considered, they were totally indifferent to **Federal Rule 11** which requires legal pleadings to be grounded in fact and verified before filing. The internal affairs division's failure to produce a court order, a probable cause affidavit, and the date for an inventory hearing required in wire tape cases were clear violations of Federal WireTap and Pen Register laws. Both the City Attorney who filed the May 31, 2018 document and the Federal Judge Hughes who approved the document were aware that the document was fraudulent prior to its filing. I believe that the filing of the August 1, 2022 ruling is published as part of a continuing smear campaign to assail my reputation.

CHAPTER THREE

FRAUD ON THE COURT BY JUDGE LYNN HUGHES CASE NO. 4:20-CV-03740

Historically, black men and women are disproportionately represented in the correctional facilities across this great country. Our quest for fairness, equality, and equity seems to be hijacked by biased police officers, an overzealous prosecutor, or a contemptuous Judge. In this chapter, I introduce you to Federal Judge Lynn Hughes, who presides over cases in the Federal Southern District Court in Houston. The Houston Southern District is part of the Fifth Circuit which covers Texas, Louisiana, and Mississippi.

In 1994, Judge Hughes presided over the [same police affirmative action lawsuit] that I was promoted from. For clarification of the record, my test scores placed me on both the regular promotional list and the affirmative action promotional list. My colleagues informed me that I would have been promoted on either list. The drama began when a B/F sergeant who scored 70 the bare minimum on one exam and failed many others concocted a scheme to frame me with domestic violence since I was going through a divorce. The internal affairs division conducted an investigation which resulted in a dismissal of the complaint due to insufficient evidence. I suspected that my ex-wife was the complainant based on her threats that she could make me lose my job because I was a black man. Coming from the Midwest, I knew women but I knew nothing about Louisiana women. The B/F sergeant saw the affirmative action promotion as her last opportunity to get promoted. When several co-workers informed me that the B/F sergeant and my ex-wife were trying to get me disqualified, I wrote the Chief of Police a letter explaining the plot. The Chief of Police promoted me. However, there was still the problem of discovering that $4 million dollars of the tax payers monies were being stolen by officers filling out phony overtime slips.

For the record, the officers who informed me of the plot were white, the officers who tried to have me disqualified were black and the Captain who said I was acting erratic at work was White. My comment regarding the diversity issue was that race was a factor but so was character. As a result of questioning why there was no internal affairs investigation of the $4 million dollars, the retaliation continued. I provided documentation in the court record to show the systemic pattern of theft from the budget and that the fact that the internal affairs division allowed the police officers who were stealing to destroy the phony overtime slips so IAD could be able to file criminal charges.

As I mentioned, I retired in 2004 but I still was unable to find employment in law enforcement. On May 1, 2018, I requested another open record search from the police department. On May 31, 2018, I received said government record claiming a criminal investigation but no complainant and no offense. I filed another open record request on May 28, 2020, and received a June 11, 2020 email from **Kim Coyne,** an open record clerk, claiming that my ex-wife made a complaint but not a police report against me. I was shocked when I received both documents from the City of Houston. These records had been denied me for three decades. Based on this information, I filed a civil rights lawsuit against the City of Houston on or about Nov. 4, 2020.

At one hearing, I believe on May 5, 2021, , Judge Hughes asked me if he checked the county records how many women would he find that I **assaulted.** I told him none. During the same hearing, Judge Hughes told me in court that I needed to stop smoking those cigarettes. I took his comments to mean marijuana. I have never tried marijuana. Based on his personal attacks, I filed a motion to have him recused because I believed that he would not be impartial. I also filed a judicial misconduct complaint against Judge Hughes and the Judicial Committee refused to sanction him.

In this chapter, the author will describe some of the retaliatory acts and the direct and circumstantial evidence supporting this miscarriage of justice. I will also show how Judge Hughes used his knowledge of the law and federal procedures to dismantle my lawsuit. Since I was unable to secure employment in Houston, my cousin invited me to come to Las Vegas to finish my testing and doctorate work. I leased out my home and headed to Las Vegas. When I was testing for my comprehensive exam to move to my Phd. dissertation in Las Vegas, my studies were interrupted when I received a notice in the mail that my home located at 17310 Beaver Spring which I had leased out **went into foreclosure.** The tenant, **Miki Barker,** texted me and told me two HPD investigators came to my home and spoke very negatively about me. These officers told her to stop paying the lease payment which triggered the foreclosure. These text messages (2010) have been entered into the court record. I had to put everything in storage, pay the delinquent mortgages, and head back to Houston to evict the tenant. One of the silver lining of this retaliatory act was that the movers miraculously retrieved some government records that refuted the lies that the Internal Affairs Division had placed in my file without my knowledge to deny me employment.

This next episode confirmed that Judge Hughes made false statement in his written court orders which were made to support the fraudulent August 1, 2022 legal ruling. As mentioned, during the May 5, 2021 hearing, I presented to Judge Hughes the email from the open records clerk, Kim Coyne aka Kimberly. The presentation of the email to Judge Hughes in open court which was captured in the court transcripts on pages 20-21. On **September 13, 2021**, Judge Hughes engaged in a blatant miscarriage of justice when he wrote up an order stating that there was no open record clerk named Kim Coyne. On October 4, 2023, the same open records clerk, **Kim Coyne,** that Judge Hughes stated didn't exist, forwarded me an email regarding **my F-5 personnel** request under PO 59197-092523.

As I mentioned, a center piece of Judge Hughes dismantling my lawsuit was the May 31, 2018 document. It is common knowledge that court orders for wiretaps and pen registers orders are signed by a Federal Judge and stored with the Clerk's Office of the Federal Courts. Based on that knowledge, once the City of Houston introduced the May 31, 2018 document referencing a criminal investigation using wiretaps and pen registers, Judge Hughes automatically knew that the **May 31, 2018 document was fabricated** because there was no record. And as part of my due diligence under a claim of fraudulent concealment against the City of Houston, I presented the May 31, 2018 document to a FBI agent, who claimed that the May 31, 2018 document was fabricated. Both Judge Hughes and the Fifth Circuit Judges ignored this material evidence deposited in the Court's record. This letter was included in the court record but was removed on multiple occasions.

Next, Judge Hughes violated a key element of a successful 42 USC 1983 federal claim against a municipality. For example, **In Piotrowski v. City of Houston, (2001)**, case no. 98-21032, the fifth circuit judges laid out the legal requirements for a successful 1983 claim. In this case, Piotrowski, a female, who got pregnant by her boyfriend who didn't want the baby. Piotrowski insisted on having the baby anyway. As a result, a conspiracy was launched to persuade her to abort the baby. This code of silence conspiracy lead to Piotrowski being shot and rendered a paraplegic by a hit man hired by her boyfriend, Richard Minns. The evidence also connected members of the Houston Police and Fire Departments to Minns and his hired investigator Dudley Bel. Minns used the services of two members of the Houston Police Department and one member of the Houston Fire Department to harass and eventually shoot Piotrowski. There are aspects of this case that are similar to mine because in the Piotrowski case, police officers concocted false charges against her to discredit her prior to the shooting. Piotrowski filed a complaint with HPD IAD and they did nothing. On Oct. 20, 1980, she was shot four times while she was sitting in her car. Despite this known misconduct, the City of Houston attorneys dismissed her case claiming that she didn't have enough evidence to state a claim. Piotrowski's counter argument was that the Houston Police **Code of Silence** contributed to the concealment of evidence in her case which resulted in the City dismissing her case. As in my case, the **moving force** responsible for Piotrowski's injury was the approval of Police Chiefs and Mayors allowing police misconduct to operate under the Houston Police Code of Silence. Under a code of silence, it is common knowledge that police will not conduct a thorough investigation of the crimes committed by a fellow officer or if an investigation is conducted it will be diminished.

The Fifth circuit identified the following legal requirements to satisfy a 1983 civil rights claims under color of law. According to the Fifth Circuit, a 1983 claim must include the following: **(1) an engaged policy maker,** (2) a constitutional violation, and (3) a custom or policy as the moving force causing the constitutional violation. Judge Hughes was aware of these legal requirements. Yet, despite his knowledge of the law and knowing that Mayor Turner had his administration draft the fabricated May 31, 2018 letter, Judge Hughes removed Mayor Turner. Also included in the evidence was my 2016 letter asking for name clearing hearing from Mayor Turner. The **removal of Mayor Turner** from the lawsuit was a violation of federal rule 19. **Federal Rule 19** determines whether an individual is necessary to the claims set forth in the complaint and whether the absence of such an individual will result in the case being dismissed because no relief can be sought without that person. Judge Hughes drafted a court order removing Mayor Sylvester Turner for arbitrary reasons which denied me a fair trial.

At the May 5, 2021 hearing, Judge Hughes stated that there was no such thing as a police code of silence and that the concept was borrowed from the movies. Once again, Judge Hughes made an inaccurate statement based on past lawsuits citing the Houston police **code of silence**. In 1995, Sharp v. City of Houston, 164 F. 3d. at 935, the Fifth Circuit recognized that the Houston Police Department operated by a police code of silence where officers were instructed by their superiors not to report police misconduct. In 2015, Zamora v. City of Houston, 798 F. 3d. at 333; Zamora testified that the Houston Police Department retaliates against officers who do report police misconduct.

In Trimmer –Davis v. City of Houston, (2020) No. 01-19-00088, expert witness and former police chief, Melvin Tucker, testified that the Houston Police Department operates by a **code of silence** as its custom. In a more recent case, Howard v. City of Houston, 4:21-cv-01179, plaintiff attorney presented into evidence that 450 HPD officers have been involved in the killings or wounding of civilians since January 1, 2004 and not one HPD officer had been indicted by an investigation conducted by the Houston Police Internal Affairs. As the plaintiff in pending federal lawsuit(s), I had entered into evidence material supporting the Howard v. City of Houston (2021) data which was researched by the Houston Chronicle. Judge Hughes knowingly and intentionally failed to take judicial notice of existing case law.

In my case, there is the issue **disparate treatment.** I was told by witnesses that IAD showed them a photo of me at home. I have not seen the photo. And I know, I didn't grant my ex-wife permission to give it to IAD. Without receiving notification of the complaint, I had no knowledge of the photo nor could I clear my name. I was vulnerable to the internal affairs division using the photo and their own false narrative to hijack my due process rights. This violation of my constitutional rights was ratified by City Leaders and previous Police Chiefs. How I was treated by IAD and Mayor Turner was the opposite of how Chief Acevedo was treated. Public information in a lawsuit revealed that this Chief was sued for receiving oral sex from a subordinate while working in Internal Affairs during time with the California Highway Patrol. Why was my photo at home be disseminated to the community but his photo at work not disseminated to the Houston Community during the police chief application process.

Judge Hughes continued to make decisions that conflicted with established legal theory and procedures. For instance, I requested a **findings of facts and conclusions of law** to understand his dismissal of my case and why I was denied a jury trial. Because of the bench trial, I requested under Texas Rule of Civil Procedure 296 as well as Federal Rule of Civil Procedure 52 to finding of facts and conclusions of law. According to the Fifth Circuit, a finding of facts and conclusion of laws is required to serve as a guide post in examining issues on appeal. Yet, Judge Hughes provided no such findings of facts and conclusions of laws and the Fifth Circuit ratified my case dismissal without one. If the August 1, 2022 opinion was what the Fifth Circuit reasoned to be a findings of facts and conclusions of law; then, legal ruling based on fraud are void.

In an attempt to obtain documents relevant and material to my lawsuit, I filed a motion for production. Judge Hughes denied my motion and substituted an in camera review without a hearing on privilege or confidential information. After the in camera review, Judge Hughes refused to allow me to review the evidence. This evidence was referred to as exhibit one, exhibit two, and exhibit three. According to law enforcement standards, the evidence that should have been released should have included tapes, photos, court orders, probable cause affidavits, evidence hearings, offense reports/complaints, and electronic surveillance applications which should have been signed by a Judge as referenced in the May 31, 2018 government document. As stated, I never was given an opportunity to review the complaint.

In my 76 page legal brief, included under cause no. 4:23 -cv-01620, I cited a Fifth Circuit case Brown v. Thompson, 430 F. 2d. 1214 (1970), where the widow of Brown sought the officer's police file who killed her husband. The District Court denied them. The Fifth Circuit overruled the district court dismissal as an abuse of discretion and reasoned that the plaintiff had a right to discovery to show that the defendants had engaged in police misconduct. Judge Hughes failure to allow me to review my own file **violated** the rulings of four Texas Attorney Generals that indicated that police employees have a special right of access to their personnel and investigative files because there is no confidentiality or privilege thresholds to overcome. I viewed Judge Hughed law violations as an obstruction of justice.

Under Frankhausen v. Rizzo (1973), the court's duty is to balance the public interest in matters of confidentiality of government information against the needs of a party to obtain records and evidence that is not otherwise available to him. Judge Hughes and the 5th Circuit were aware that my pleading for records was flanked by a claim of fraudulent concealment of relevant and material evidence. As a discovery guide, Frankhausen v. Rizzo (1973), provided Judge Hughes with ten concerns in granting confidential records to the party requesting them or denying them. Rather than cite all ten, I incorporated those that are significant to my lawsuit: (2) the impact on individuals for having their identities disclosed, (4) whether, the information sought is factual, (6) whether the police investigation is complete, (8) whether suit is bought in good faith, (9) whether the information sought is available through other sources, and (10) the importance of the information sought. As evidence previously presented, the May 5, 1995 and May 8, 1995 government documents indicated that a criminal investigation was conducted and dismissed due to insufficient evidence and there was no administrative personnel concerns program; so why did Judge Hughes deny me the documents in exhibit 1, exhibit 2, and exhibit 3 as referenced in the May 31, 2018 City of Houston document. Without the ability to examine the above exhibits, this author is convinced that Judge Hughes lied about the existence of the evidence because there was none. I believe such acts are egregious and unacceptable.

In Wood v. Breier, 54 F.R.D. 7 (E.D. Wisc. 1972), the Judge [Reynolds] conducted an in camera review of a police file under a [discovery challenge] and commented that 42 USC 1983 civil right claims should be resolved by a **determination of the truth rather than a determination that the truth be hidden.** Judge Hughes and the Fifth Circuit were only concerned with hiding the truth. According to the May 31, 2018 letter, the prosecutor under Brady v. Maryland, 373 U.S. 83, 87, 10, Ed. 2d. 215, 83 S. Ct. 1194 (1963), had to release any evidence that was favorable or material to guilt or punishment of the accused. In January 2024, I submitted an open record request to the Harris County District Attorney's requesting domestic violence police complaints and or reports from 1994 to January 12, 2024. Their investigation revealed that the Houston Police Department Internal Affairs Division **never** filed any complaints or reports against me to the Harris County's DA's Office. This document has been placed in the court record as evidence.

By denying this author government records material to his lawsuit, Judge Hughes also violated **Federal Rule Code of Procedure 56** which allows summary judgment only when there is no evidence, no facts, and no affidavits in the record which support the claims of the moving party. I presented a preponderance of evidence to support my claims. However, Judge Hughes still dismissed his case under a summary judgment. During the May 6, 2021 hearing, I informed Judge Hughes that the City of Houston had violated the **Police Officers Bill of Rights** under the Texas Local Government Code, 143.123 which stated police officers have a right to receive a copy of any complaints filed against them. Under the sixth amendment, I had a right to confront any witness or accuser making allegations against me (Converse v. City of Kemah, Civil Action 3:15 –cv-00105 (2020). In another case, Coughlin v. Lee, 946 F. 2d., 1152, 1159 (5 Cir. 1991), the fifth circuit defines the law enforcement privilege as "a qualified privilege protecting investigative files in an ongoing investigation (ROA.1295). Both Judge Hughes and the City Attorney knew that the 1994 case was closed. At the May 7, 2021 hearing, the City Attorney, Majorie Cohen stated that the 94-1649 investigation was not sustained (ROA.1405:9-10) and closed. So why hasn't the City of Houston released the investigative file to me since the case was closed since 1995?

On April 21, 2021 , I submitted an affidavit based on a conversation with a retired lieutenant familiar with IAD procedures. This retired lieutenant stated that IAD keeps a file of records written on 3 by 5 cards which are used as a dirty file to discredit police officers, politicians, and community leaders. In an effort to dismantle my lawsuit, JudgeHughes also struck my use of John Doe as a placeholder until the officer's identity became known though discovery.

As I continued to include Texas case law relating to discovery, Judge Hughes continued to ignore the law. In Gallaher v. City of Maypearl, Civic Action No. 3: 17 –cv-1400-M (nD.Tex. Feb. 2, 2018): the Judge in that case wrote, "In the context of municipal liability, as opposed to individual officer liability, it is exceedingly rare that a plaintiff will have access to (or personal knowledge of) specific details regarding the existence or absence of internal policies or training procedures prior to discovery". In my motion for production, I requested existing policies and procedures for handling citizen complaints and retention policies for closed cases according to state law. This author believes that the reason for Judge Hughes' efforts to dismantle his lawsuit was because he was frustrated with a black man questioning his authority. In essence, I didn't act like I knew my place.

Over a span of three decades, the retaliation didn't cease. Under case law, Beckwith at 4* (5 Circuit Oct. 16, 2019) (quoting Gen. Universal Sys. Inc. v. Hal, Inc., 500 F.3d. 444, 451 (5 Circuit. 2007), the continuing tort theory is used to explain the continuation of injury and harms of a similar nature to a person can be charged as well as previous acts of harm to the person until the last wrongful act stops. I was terminated from my last job at PUE LLC and PUE Energy because I would not drop my lawsuit against the City of Houston. Ms Joaquina Spikes Winslow was working with the Houston Police Department IAD and politicians on her energy project.

On **March 6, 2022,** Joaquina Spikes aka Winslow informed retired HPD sergeant A. Jefferson that she had told me that I needed to drop my complaints against City of Houston and the Police Department or be terminated.. On f March 10, 2022, Spikes aka Winslow made a false police report that I stole her intellectual property to the Pearland

Police Officer [Sears]. Despite Ms. Joaquina Spikes Winslow **using money from numerous clients** to pay her bills and **not showing up for Court to answer this lawsuit,** the current Judge has taken no action to rule on my default judgment motion before the Court. I believe the failure to enter a default judgment when a defendant does not appear or answer the complaint is a clear a double standard. I worked a whole year under contract. I'm still waiting to be compensated. My last employer claims that she is politically protected. Based on the delay of the default judgment motion ruling, is the current Federal Judge violating the law too.

Prior to filing this lawsuit, I reached an all time low when I discovered that on **July 26, 2019**, the internal affairs division or an officer Vasquez in Major Offenders contacted my son, Martice Hall and told him that he had an outstanding criminal warrant on him. This was not true but it was part of the retaliation aimed at me for not dropping my complaints, grievances, and lawsuit. My son was given a phony case number 940808-196. The phone number was 713-308-3152. My son also called an attorney named, Guy Womack at 832-654-0382. My son told me that Officer Vasquez was a female officer and slandered me to him. Officer Vasquez told my son that I pulled a gun on Malveaux and Guillory. I received no police complaints on either one of these allegations to clear my name and has not been afforded the opportunity to place either woman on the witness stand under oath. My son became paranoid and stopped his dialysis treatments. **My son died.** This was an all time low for me. I blamed myself for his death because the internal affairs division used him to retaliate against me. I made a complaint to HPD and the Sheriff Department to investigate the threat of a bogus criminal warrant by Officer Vasquez as an act of official oppression. Neither agency conducted an investigation of this criminal matter. This act occurred on the watch of Chief Acevedo and Mayor Slyvester Turner as well as the May 31, 2018 fabricated government record.

CHAPTER FOUR

A NEW LAWSUIT – SAME STIGMA PLUS NARRATIVE

As mentioned in the letter to the U.S. Attorney Alameda S. Hamdani, the next employment episode occurred on Oct. 3, 2022 at the Houston Police Gun Range when I went to obtain my official Houston Police Identification card. I had already qualified under the Texas Law Enforcement Commission requirements but I needed to pick up my Houston Police Identification Card. At the gun range, **Officer Cromwell informed me that my payroll was flagged with personnel administrative concerns** negative information and that **I needed an approval from the new police attorney, Ursula Williams. I was told that my payroll had been flagged since 1995. I said this is crazy.** I informed Officer Cromwell that the information was false and that information was referencing an incident which I never participated in. The May 5, 1995 letter from the City of Houston confirmed that. So why was my name being stigmatized 30 years later.

Discovering that my payroll had been flagged was significant because it provided the missing piece to the stigma plus conspiracy. For twenty nine years, **I had complained to elected officials Democrats and Republicans, Attorneys, Pastors, Civil Rights Organizations, and Community Leaders** that I was unable to obtain employment due to a tainted criminal investigation by IAD. Each time that I made a complaint, the internal affairs division would present the alleged photo of me at home and make allegations of domestic violence without my knowledge. None of these well educated people asked the question where was my answer to the complaints made against me. I believe no one was concerned about my career because any public attention to me would trigger questions about the $4 million dollars stolen by police and politicians and raise such questions as: 1) why was there not an internal affairs investigation, 2) who instructed the bogus overtime slips to be destroyed, and 3) who was the City Controller. I believe that the internal affairs division was instructed to continue the smear campaign against me as the distraction and justification for not asking the investigative questions about the stolen $4 million dollars. The City of Houston's code of silence was invoked to protect those politicians who benefitted from receiving kickbacks of the stolen tax payers money.

In order to cover up the stolen $4 million dollars overtime scheme, City officials instructed IAD to continue claiming that I was delusional or a serial domestic violence abuser. In order to prove that the Internal Affairs Division was using the alleged photo and their own false narrative without giving me an opportunity to clear my name, I contacted the District Attorney's Office. On **Dec. 2, 2023,** Harris County District Attorney Kim Ogg stated no claims for domestic violence were ever made against me from 1994 to present (see evidence in record) by the Houston Police Department or any other law enforcement agency. This official piece of evidence proved that the reputation harm done to my career was intentionally done by the internal affairs division with the approval of police department, the City of Houston, and the Courts to protect other politicians. Several of these politicians were Hispanic.

The Oct. 3, 2022 incident at the gun range confirmed the stigma plus smear campaign had been going on since 1995 based on the administrative personnel concern alert affixed to my payroll. I was flagged as delusional and mentally unfit. As I would fill out police employment applications with other agencies, those applications would have a section pertaining to domestic violence. Because I would answer those questions in the negative, the new employers were convinced that I was lying once they contacted HPD internal affairs division. This corrupt system worked for 30 years because the City of Houston officials were involved in the cover up.

Despite the evidence and findings of the May 5, 1995 and the May 8, 1995 City of Houston correspondences which were retrieved from the Las Vegas storage bin claiming that these matters were terminated, Judge Hughes and the Fifth Circuit ignored this evidence and used the claim that I was delusional to protect those police chiefs and public officials who participated in the the money grab of taxpayers monies. Throughout my story, you the reader will see patterns of this scheme to defraud tax payers via phony overtime and kickback schemes. I was denied a jury trial by Judge Hughes so the public would not be alerted to the scheme that elected officials sanctioned and participated in. In response to the new evidence and new lawsuit, the City of Houston filed motions to dismiss this lawsuit on 12(b)(1), 12(b)(6), and res judicata motions in an effort to cover up the new stigma plus evidence discovered at the gun range on Oct. 3, 2022. The next chapter addresses these motions.

CHAPTER FIVE

THE EXCEPTION TO RES JUDICATA IS FRAUD

Integrity is always about aligning theory to practice. In this case study, I will show that the City of Houston and Judge Hughes conspired to violate multiple laws. The most serious of these violations was the fabrication of the May 31, 2018 document which was used to cover up the initial illegal criminal investigation which was designed to frame me. This act alone was enough to put any common criminal in jail for obstructing justice.

Yet, the conspiracy to obstruct justice and to deprive me of my civil rights continued with the publication of the August 1, 2022 legal opinion. If the truth of proposition B is dependent on the truth of proposition A; then, if A is false, so is B in a normal world. But the circumstances that I have been describing are not typical of a normal world. These circumstances are characterized by politics where one plus one equals three rather than two. Because the May 31, 2018 document was assessed by an FBI agent to be fabricated, the document was removed from the court record or not included on several occasions. I had to put it back. During the appeal process, I placed it in the evidence section of the record excerpt so all evidence, motions, and error orders could be reviewed by the three Judge panel. On August 1, 2022, the three Judge Panel of the 5th Circuit affirmed the fraudulent ruling and published it as if it was true in order to cover up the City of Houston criminal act of tampering with a government record. In general, a claim for res judicata means that the two lawsuits that I filed are the same and any claims brought forth in the second lawsuit are non-actionable because they should have been raised in the previous lawsuit.

Briefly, the City of Houston's res judicata motion is flawed for the following three reasons:
1) Their argument against me is based on slander, gossip, and defamation of character,
2) Their argument is based on the City of Houston submitting and filing the fabricated May 31, 2018 government record which a Houston FBI agent verified as fabricated and
3) Their argument omits their intentional efforts to conceal documents from the hearing and
4) Their arguments contradicts Supreme Court law, statutory law, and case law which grant a police officer their right to review and inspect what has been placed in his personnel and internal affairs file for defense purposes and privacy interest.

The City of Houston filed these motions knowing that the disputed records were still concealed from this author's examination. This author claims that the above motions were part of the City's continuing theory to deprive him of his constitutional rights.

CHAPTER SIX

THE FAILURE TO INVESTIGATE UNDER THE POLICE AND JUDICIAL CODE OF SILENCE

A central theme in this lawsuit is that the police code of silence which is essentially a conspiracy of silence that deprives a citizen of his or her Constitutional Rights. The code's purpose is to conceal any kind of misconduct. The misconduct does not have to be criminal in nature. It can be civil in terms of fraud, waste, and or the mismanagement of an organizations financial resources which leads to sub-optimization of performance and or services rendered or delivered. When the code of silence is practiced by police or judicial organizations, it is synonymous with an intentional failure to investigate the misconduct in order to protect the violator(s) who knowingly violate rules, policies, procedures, and laws.

The code takes on various forms in policing and in courts. Some of these forms include: [obstructing justice], witness tampering, producing fabricated evidence, destroying evidence, concealing damaging information, suborning perjury, committing perjury, violating laws, violating due process procedures, concealing records, defamation, fraud, conducting diminished investigations and preparing false police reports. In terms of organizational culture, the code of silence flourishes where: "double standards", a "We" versus "Them" mentality exist, Secrecy, Superior v. Inferior psychological conditioning, and corrupt intentions exist.

By failing to investigate, the corrupt party secures an unfair advantage at the expense of the other party. In the present case, the City of Houston obtained an unfair advantage in Court by concealing a tainted criminal investigation from this author which was used to stigmatize his reputation and deny him employment. By denying him employment, he was unable to hire competent counsel and pay his federal student loans which he also complained about to the Secretary of Education. As a consequence of Judge Hughes failing to investigate the fabricated evidence produced by the City, he engaged in a conflict of interest with respect to his duties of impartiality as a Federal Judge which resulted in denying me a fair trial and violating the following constitutional rights: first amendment-freedom of speech and a right to petition the government, fourth amendment-illegal search and seizures, sixth amendment-right to confront accusers, seventh amendment -Right to a Jury trial , fifth amendment (equal protection of the law and double jeopardy), and fourteenth amendment-notice and due process. Given Judge Hughes remarks that I needed to stop smoking those cigarettes was an indication that Judge Hughes had engaged in some degree of ex parte community with possibly the Houston Police internal affairs which was a violation of the judicial code of misconduct because those conversations were outside of court and not under oath. Yet, this was the defamation tactic used by IAD for 30 years. No one mentioned my nine commendations for outstanding police work.

On March 10, 2022, Joaquina Winslow aka Joaquina Spikes aka Joaquina aka Sykes informed the Pearland Police that I was terminated because I stole her intellectual property and five of her employees witnessed the theft. This claim was part of a joint conspiracy between HPD IAD, Winslow, and the Pearland Police Department. IAD told Spikes and Pearland PD what they told Judge Hughes, which was that I was delusional. No one mentioned that I possessed two Masters degrees and a Phd. Nor did anyone care. No one cared because I was fighting a corrupt system and I was perceived as a threat.

While the consensus of the defendants was that I was delusional, there was an unexpected change in the case that confirmed my law enforcement suspicions that my old boss, Joaquina Spikes aka Joaquina Winslow was engaged in fraudulent behavior. On January 15, 2024, I received a **call** from six participants of Joaquina Winslow aka Joaquina Spikes aka Joaquina Sykes **grant program.** These individuals claimed that **Spikes had defrauded them** and **stole their money** without reimbursing them. These individuals traveled from Louisiana and Mississippi to bring their affidavits and business records to file under my lawsuit. They told me that Spikes had lied on me and **claimed that I was delusional**; this news was evidence of the tactic used by the Houston Police Internal Affairs Division as well as the recent discovery of my payroll being flagged from 1995 to Oct. 3, 2022.

Among all affidavits and documents filed, one document placed in the court's record which was written by Spikes and shared by the Germany family, stood out. The Germany family was given a guarantee letter to take to their bank in the amount of $2.5 million dollars. Joaquina Spikes aka Joaquina Winslow informed them that her Pure Urban Excellent bank or trust would transfer the money immediately from her bank to theirs. Of course, their banker kicked them out of his bank citing fraud. The Germany family produced receipts showing that they gave Joaquina Spikes aka Winslow $28,000 dollars for grant program training in exchange for a million dollar grant. At the time that Ms. Winslow was introduced to me, I didn't vet her because my friend was Military and vouched for her character. When I began to observe conflicting behavior, I began my own investigation and I was terminated.

CHAPTER SEVEN

BREAKING THE CODE OF SILENCE

In this chapter, I talk about breaking the code of silence. To do so, I preface my comments with several biblical verses to lay a foundation that is necessary for our understanding that the code of silence is an ungodly instrument used to maintain a corrupt organization and therefore, spiritual warfare is necessary to defeat it. Because the code represents the suppression and obstruction of the truth, we are dealing with the character issue of a corrupt spirit. In Proverbs 11:20, it says that "The Lord detests those who hearts are perverse, but he delights in those whose ways are blameless". In Titus 1:7-8, Paul provides instruction to Titus regarding leadership within the Church: he or she must be blameless, not overbearing, not quick tempered, not given to drunkenness, not violent, not pursuing dishonest gain. In Micah 3:9-11, Micah rebukes Judges and Leaders who distort what is right, those who judge for a bribe, those who teach for a price, and prophets who tell fortunes for money. This scripture addresses those who claim to serve God while engaging in corrupt practices.

Adding to these scriptures are several borrowed from a Utube presentation dated Feb. 2, 2022, of a sermon by the late Pastor, Fred K.C. Price. In Romans 13: Verse 1-2, reads "Let everyone be subject to the governing authorities, for there is no authority except that which God has established. Those who rebel will bring judgment on themselves." In Samuel 16 verse 7, God says do not look at a person's outer appearance but the Lord looks at the person's heart. In Timothy 5 verse 21, the scripture reminds us to observe things without prejudice, do nothing with partiality. In John 5 verse 17 all unrighteousness is sin. In Mathew 23: 23, "Woe to you, teachers of the law and Pharisees, you hypocrites! You give a tenth of your spices -mint, dill and cumin. But you have neglected the more important matters of the law -justice, mercy, and faithfulness. You should have practiced the latter, without neglecting the former". In Galatians 2 verses 11-14, this scripture references an incident where Paul criticizes Peter for his **hypocrisy** in withdrawing from eating with Gentile Christians when Jewish Christians arrived. Paul's criticism highlights the importance of consistency and integrity in living out the principles of the gospel. Also, Paul emphasized the importance of **public criticism** so that the offender would be accountable to the public. The following verses represent Godly concepts that support a healthy police or judicial institution. The defendants in my lawsuit strayed away from the laws that they were appointed to defend. These individuals forgot that God exalts men and also brings them down. Psalm 75: 6-7.

With respect to the code of silence, cops are practical individuals. They for the most part are trained to operate from a stimulus response format. If an officer or officers engage in the code of silence, its because they are using their social brain which supports group acceptance and conformity. They learn early in their careers to conform and adopt a "We" versus "Them" mentality. On the other hand, police chiefs encourage officers to participate in the code of silence and the "rotten apple" theory which is nothing more than a self-serving facade used by police chiefs to cover up their approval of police misconduct (Trautman, N. 2000). In the current case, Judges Hughes engaged in the code of silence to protect his political friends and colleagues.

I have continuously stated based on the evidence or lack of evidence in this case that the City of Houston and the Police Department engaged in economic retaliation based on racial and political animus. The disparate treatment that I have experienced over the past 30 years has been comparable to the same opposition that Dr. King experience when he drew attention to civil rights injustices and economic injustices of poor people. What happen to me was a wrong that happened 30 years ago, and people have thought that I'm crazy for presenting the truth. I tried to present it sooner but the code of silence prevented others from speaking out of fear.

This fear is not imaginary. I recall a fellow Lieutenant named Mabry. **In 1995**, Lt Mabry was found dead by a gunshot to the head. Lt. Mabry had discovered that officers at the police pension were stealing thousands of dollars and announced that he was going to report it to the news media. The next morning before the meeting, he had been stalked and murdered. Ray Hill, a local Prison Show host, made the comment: "Cops lie, cheat and steal", "They will kill in cold blood and get away with it". The type of policing by the Houston Police has been pathologic in nature for decades. Correcting the problem begins with their code of silence. Lt. Mabry was white.

Historically, the Houston Police Department has had a long history of policing under a banner of Jim Crow laws as far back as 1917 when black soldiers were court martial for participating in a race riot when a black soldier intervened in the physical assault of a black woman being beaten by a white Houston Police Officer at Camp Logan. On August 23, 1917, the race riot resulted in the deaths of police officers, soldiers, and citizens. Through the work of a South Texas College of Law School, Attorney Ashley Cromika, and Catherine Greene Burnett, of the Innocent Project, the court martials of the 110 soldiers were overturned on November 13, 2023 by the U.S. Army. Attorney Cromika stated that a project of this magnitude takes a village to research. The researcher went over 2,500 pages of transcripts to find evidence that soldiers didn't receive a fair trial. One lawyer represented 60 soldiers. Many soldiers were 15 years of age and only had a 4th grade education. Attorney Cromika stated that these soldiers wanted to serve their country and be treated like soldiers. For the soldiers who were executed, their military record read, "terminated by death without honor". For Afro Americans, this theme of serving one's country with distinction despite being treated like second class citizens is always worthy of recognition in spite of the Jim Crow mentality that we have been subjected to.

In 1977, a Houston native, a U.S. Army veteran, was a victim of police brutality. The beating and murder of Sergeant Jose Campos Torres was one of the most notorious examples of police misconduct. The guilty officers were convicted of violating his civil rights but only received a one-year prison sentence. On May 5, 1977, Torres was arrested after an altercation with a local bar owner. He was handcuffed by the police and on route to the city jail. Officers C. Eugene Elliott,

Jerome Skolnick, and Stephen Orlando made a detour and transported him to the **hole, a secret spot** along Buffalo Bayou where cops often took prisoners whom they wanted to beat up before taking them to jail. Officers Terry Wayne Denson, Joseph Janish, Louis Kinney, and Glenn Brinkmeyer joined them at the hole. After severely beating Torres, they took him to the City Jail but were ordered to take him to Ben Taub Hospital instead. Instead of taking Torres to the Hospital, they took him back to the "hole" for a second beating. They took Torres to the Bayou where he drowned from the beatings. When the sergeant asked where Torres was, the officers stated that he was released. But a rookie officer, Eugene Elliot, **broke the code of silence** when he told his father, a former police officer, what really happen. The Torres Family filed a missing person report and three days later, Jose Campos Torres body was founded in Buffalo Bayou. The Houston Chief of Police, Bryon Glenn Bond, created the Internal Affairs Division, before he resigned (Texas Monthly). In October 2023, The Baton Rouge Police Department, was cited in a police brutality case for taking suspects to a **vacant warehouse** where officers physically assaulted suspects; the hole and the warehouse are both police practices that come under the umbrella of the code of silence.

HPD has a history of stealing money from citizens. In 1994, I reported $4 millions dollars was stolen in phony overtime slips from the jail budget. In 2008, a police officer stole $680k from the police credit union. In 2012, the Houston Chronicle conducted an internal IAD audit of officers charged with criminal offenses. The internal affairs audit revealed that there were over 250 officers who had committed criminal offenses and still [retained their employment]. I retired in 2004 based on a constructive discharge. The police department denied me the opportunity to go to the FBI academy or transfer out of the Jail. In the same year 2012, four Houston Police Officers stole over a million dollars in falsifying overtime slips made out to each other in 2012. One officer made over $375k in addition to his regular salary. The Chief of Police gave the three officers and the sergeant from 20 to 35 days off without pay. When an officer signs a bogus overtime slip, the Texas Penal Code claims such action as falsifying a government record.

In the Hardy Street scandal [2019], Houston police officers killed two innocent citizens based on a false search warrant as part of a drug raid gone bad. The police chief is [alleged] to have signed off on an inaccurate police investigation by the IAD before leaving town. In the same investigation, the DA's Office investigation revealed that six members of the Narcotic team were also engaged in a conspiracy to sign bogus overtime slips. But more important is why the IAD investigation of police misconduct was wrong. Based on the investigation of the hired forensic expert, unknown HPD Officers re-positioned the body and placed a gun in the dead woman's hand. This type of police misconduct can be attributed to the Houston Police Code of Silence.

On Feb. 20, 2024, the current Houston police chief stated that he was [unaware] that there were 4106 rape kits which had not been examined for the suspects' DNA. In response, the Chief stated he would provide additional officers to solve the problem. This is not a new problem. One of the negative consequences of a code of silence is that it intentionally conceals information from the tax paying public. Historically, the current rape kit problem is a carry over from 2015 scandal. What the Chief didn't say was that there were other divisions where a lack of manpower resulted in the same second hand trauma experienced by citizens who filed crime complaints but received no investigation and no notification. The new numbers have raised the total of un-investigated criminal cases to 260,000 since 2016.. The failure to inform the public of this kind of critical information is symptomatic of their police code of silence.

In terms of the judicial code of silence, the Houston Chronicle did a story on the reprimand by the 5th Circuit of Judge Kent in 2007. Judge Kent was impeached by Congress and the Senate for the sexually assault of several female employees whom he would threaten with employment termination if they didn't submit. The Judge reminded them of their oath of secrecy; "what happens at the court stays at the Court". The details of the case revealed that [even] a Court Security officer, who knew of the sexual assault was afraid to speak out against the Judge. In my case, Judge Lynn Hughes had seven or eight cases remanded back to the Houston Southern District by the Fifth Circuit for racial comments and procedural violations before he wrote and published the fraudulent August 1, 2022 legal opinion. In March of 2022, Judge Hughes was relegated to Senior Judge status.

The lesson learned if any is that the code of silence and the failure to investigate misconduct benefits individuals from a micro point of view; however, the code's negative effect on other institutions and our democracy contributes to our **societal regression** rather than social progress. Prior to the take over of the Houston Independent School District, all previous school trustees knew in advance that there were deficiencies in student learning. These student learning deficiencies were concealed from the public and anyone who brought attention to HISD's problems was labeled a "trouble maker" or a runaway slave. While the rational thing to do would be to acknowledge the students' skill deficiencies and fix the problem, the school leaders intentionally chose to engage in the pretext that it was another kind of problem.

In other words, the leaders engaged in "gamesmanship" to distract the public from the real problems in order to deny that they had any accountability in correcting the problem that they were appointed or elected to solve. While one set of officials weren't addressing the student skill deficiencies, the other group of officials were taking bribes of $3M and being indicted, i.e. HISD operating chief, Brian Busby (2021), and HISD school board president, Rhonda Skillern-Jones, 2022, who pled guilty to accepting a bribe as part of a kickback scheme conspiracy. The current HISD superintendent, Mike Miles, has stated that the district has spent $26 million in unmonitored administrative over time. Miles also cited waste in purchasing the fleet of buses not used. When financial information of this source is kept from the public, it is symbolic of an organization that operates by private meetings after the public meetings to find loops to ingratiate and enrich themselves at the expense of the public. A conspiracy is defined as two or more individuals engaged in a nefarious plan to achieve ill gotten gains. For this kind of financial mismanagement to be concealed, someone had to violate their fiduciary duty to inform the public.

In order to break the code of silence cycle, Leaders must view the code from a macro perspective and anticipate the deleterious effect on other institutions which impact the community's ecosystem. A failure to take a systems approach to the code of silence should result in the immediate removal of that leader. Once compromised, these individuals become more seasoned/callous/contemptuous/indurate as the time goes by since their concealment reinforces a mindset that

BREAKING THE CODE OF SILENCE

I don't have to be accountable to anyone. Participating in the code of silence means violating the **privilege ....**to serve the public.

According to Albert Einstein , "you can't expect the people who created the problem to come up with a solution". In breaking the Code of Silence, HPD can accept my police training and also employ external audits by such groups as CALEA which represents the Commission on Accreditation for Law Enforcement Agencies which is a neutral party that will come in and audit the Houston Police Department to evaluate if their policies, procedures, and practices are attune with national law enforcement best practices. For Federal Judges, neuroscience testing with fmri can measure neural activity in the brain based on blood and oxygen flow to areas of the brain that have been stimulated by an object or person. In cases of racial prejudices and lying, the functional magnetic resonance imaging can be used to detect areas of the brain that **reveal these anomalies.**

CONCLUSION

LEAVING THE PLANTATION MINDSET

Growing up poor, I could have let my circumstances determine my development…but I didn't. My dad had a 4th grade education but he extended his learning in the military. He would ask each of us what did we learn in school and you better not say nothing. When he was murdered in Chicago, I felt helping disadvantaged minorities like me was my assignment and law enforcement would allow me to do that. I earned my reputation and my integrity in the streets, in sports, and intellectually in everything that I did. So when a "good old boy" on the Houston Police Department told me that I didn't know my place, I said, nigger please. This exchange was more about Houston than me. As the fourth largest City in the United States, Houston was still stuck in a segregated mindset in the 1990s; as evidenced by the KKK flyer placed in my apartment door jam.

As an institution, law enforcement is characterized by a similar mindset. It is a mindset that grew out of slavery where runaway slaves were hunted by "patroller' or "patrolmen". This hierarchy of freemen and slaves was a social culture based on the belief that whites were more superior intellectually than blacks. These beliefs lead to a social structure where whites constructed the "slave codes" to remind slaves of their place. Slaves needed travel passes and their owner's permission to go anywhere. This was the tactic used by the internal affairs division when they flagged my payroll until I discovered it in 2022. Slaves were forbidden to learn how to read and write. Without an excellent education, HISD students can't compete on a global scale.

For 29 years, the Houston Police Department treated me as their slave. The police without authorization would access my personal data from my pension records to monitor my civilian activity.

The relationship between the "slave codes" and the "police code of silence" are one of the same. Both the "slave codes" and the "police code of silence" served the same purpose of maintaining and applying the control over those who are perceived as "less valued" by those in power or those who wish to be in power. Historically, the police code of silence originated from the "slave codes". This note was made by Lou Reiter, a Police Chief and Legal Scholar, who trains officers in setting up IAD Divisions and testifies on matters such as the police code of silence. Today, when officers engage in covering up police misconduct, they are morphing the same behavior that Southern whites used against slaves during the most horrific periods of American history.

After slaves were freed, the Klan still terrorized free black men, women, and children. After I left HPD in 2004, the internal affairs division still retaliated against me by flagging my payroll to give me a negative reference. The acts of retaliation after I left the department bewildered me. I left so what more do you want. This was the same state of bewilderment that slaves felt when their slave owner would beat them half to death and then use religion to justify the beating. Today, the Courts have taken the place of religion. For blacks, the courts represent the rules where justice can be obtained. Yet, the empirical data states otherwise.

According to U.S. Bureau of Justice Statistics (2020), Blacks are incarcerated at a rate of 33% in comparison to their population percent of 13%.; whereas, Whites are incarcerated at a rate of 30% in comparison to their population percent of 65%. These disproportionate numbers indicate disparities caused by multiple factors. However, because of the historic slave owner and slave dichotomy, individual and institutional racism can contribute to these incarceration percentages. But there is another explanation other than race, this explanation is based on the neuroscience concept of pattern recognition and sense making. All prejudices are learned behaviors.

In my lawsuit, I verified that the City of Houston presented a government record, i.e. May 31, 2018, which City Attorneys presented in court as fabricated. In Wilson v. State, 311S.W. 3d. 452 (Tex. Criminal App. 2010), the Court decided that evidence obtained illegally violated the law and therefore was inadmissible under the code of criminal procedural Article 38.23. However, despite case law, the internal affairs division violated privacy laws and used a photo of me at home taken without my consent and interjected it into the public domain without my knowledge, as a tactic to frame and defame me. The internal affairs investigation is a public record. In State v. Vasilas, 187 S.W.3d. 486 (Tex. Crim. App. 2006), the law states that an individual violates Texas Penal Code 37.10 when they tamper with a government record if he or she makes, presents, or use a government record with knowledge of its falsification. The Pearland Police Department made a false police report claiming I stole Spike's intellectual property without investigating Spike or notifying me of the report.

In De La Paz v. State, 279 S.W.3d.336 (Tex. Crim. App. 2009), a police officer was convicted for fabricating evidence and filing a false police report. In Wingo v. State, 143 S.W.3d. 178, 187 (Tex. App. San Antonio 2004), the law prohibits police and citizens from filing a false incident report, aff'd 189 S.W.3d. 270 (Tex. Crim. App. 2006). In State v. Stephens, 608 S.W.3d. 245 (Tex. App. 2020) Section 37.10(a)(2) of the Texas Penal Code makes it an offense to make , present, or use any record, document, or thing with knowledge of its falsity and with the intent that it be taken as a genuine government record. This section of the penal code describes a government record to include "anything belonging to, received by, or kept by the government for information, including **court** records.

Despite these law and constitutional violations, a Federal Judge still dismissed the author's case. This narrative about **American Injustice** with respect to black men is not new. But what has become increasingly disturbing is that society had become so psychologically numb that they accept injustices of all kinds as normal. Our problem is that our attention has been misdirected and we have been brainwashed to believe that 90 percent of one's failure is due to some one else's race and the remaining 10 percent to your education, training, and or sweat equity. Instead of inverting the equation, we look for another scapegoat. We fail because we consent to allowing someone else to "**think for us**" and we fail because we don't have the courage to learn what we don't know. In essence, we allow our thinking to be hijacked or because we chose to be intellectually lazy.

Recently, I observed a lawsuit pertaining to the height of a black student's hair; why not style a lawsuit based on the failure to educate the student based on his zip code. **What** the white HPD officer said and **what** the Judge's actions conveyed to me was that they perceived me as having less value than them. Both were expressing their own racial conditioning. For me as a black man, everywhere I went to be validated was based on standards set by individuals who have spent a lifetime developing their minds. Privilege does exist but character trumps privilege. If you're dumb, all races recognize that. Therefore, white privilege has its limits. Race is important but **character** is far more important than race. Dr. King spoke on the virtues of character a decade preceding my generation.

On September 25, 1883, Frederick Douglas also spoke on the importance of **character.** In speaking on the character of American, he stated: Though the colored man is no longer subject to barter and sale, he is surrounded by an adverse settlement which fetters all his movement. In his downward course, he meets no resistance, but his course upward is resented and resisted at every step of his progress. If he comes in ignorance, rags and wretchedness he conforms to the popular belief of his **character**, and in that character....he is welcome; but if he shall come as a gentleman, a scholar and a statesman, he is hailed as a contradiction to the national faith concerning his race, and his coming is resented as impudence in one case he may provoke contempt and derision, **but** in the other he is an affront to pride and provokes malice. Dr. King was talking about the character issue in America in the 1960s and Dr. Frederick Douglas was talking about

America's character issue in 1883. In this book, Dr. Hall is talking about the [same] character issue(s) in America in 2024.

The time traveler element demonstrates that America doesn't have a knowledge problem: America has a **character** problem. Leaders recite words and phrases like a parrot and we approve them for being porch pirates. We allow them to recite their experiences and we confuse experiences for wisdom. Wisdom is the application of knowledge. Some people can't solve a problem because they don't have the knowledge to solve it. So they do a lot of pretending. Instead of evaluating them on their titles; we should evaluate leaders based on the application of their knowledge and their measurable results. What a leader says should align with what a leader accomplishes. Without this alignment, there's a discrepancy in the individual's integrity. An integrity driven decision is one that reflects God's trinity; the decision is made with a pure heart, a clear mind, and [capable] hands and feet.

Leaving the plantation mindset which is the subtitle of the book is injected because its' purpose is to raise the conscious level of black people to become more aware of their consensual programming dilemma. It is based on years of institutional programming which conditions Blacks to believe that they are in control of their destiny when they lack the essential resources such as a quality education to compete at higher levels. When George Floyd was killed by the police, no one would deny that this was one of many tragedies in our civil rights struggle. As a result of his death….we marched in protest. Yet, our children attend failed schools which correlate to crime but we fail to march for the education parity of black and brown children.

Leaving the plantation mindset requires us to shift our attention to the institutions that shape our communities and the " unhealthy" police culture that interacts with our communities. Because police officers are concerned with their own safety, their jaded view of society and the "us" versus "them" mentality are real. This perspective becomes unmanageable when police leaders failed to address the police code of silence and take proactive wellness measures to address the psychological numbness that all police experience. In another book, the author will discuss neuroscience training for police officers. But for now, I will point to the continual need for new training by citing several well known cases that emphasize the need for new police training. When police are conditioned to believe that its' "us" against "them", fear triggers the amygdala and rational thought becomes obscured for a split second. In the following cases, George Floyd [2020] Minneapolis, Breonna Taylor [2020] in Kentucky; Michael Brown [2014] Mississippi; Tamir Rice [2014] Ohio; Philando Castile [2016] Minnesota, and Emmett Till [1955] Mississippi, both neuroscience and race are in play in these deaths.

The plantation mindset must be changed because it allows individuals who are in positions of authority to determine [**who is worthy based on plantation mindset standards**]. This is a dangerous precipice. This is a dangerous standard because look at what has happened to our country when we substitute privilege over character and popularity over merit. Leaving the plantation mindset, requires a new kind of leader and a demolition of old obsolete ideas that do nothing to build trust in communities of color.

In the Gospel of Luke (Luke 16: 19-31), Jesus told the parable about a beggar named Lazarus and a rich man. Lazarus, who was covered with sores, lay at the gate of the rich man's house every day, asking for scraps of food from the rich man's table to sustain him. The Rich man didn't help Lazarus because he determined Lazarus wasn't worthy. Both men died. Lazarus went to heaven and the Rich man went to hell. Jesus used the parable to call attention to the Rich man's plantation mindset with respect to how (he treated others). Literary scholars stated that the Gospel of Luke 16: 19-31 was written between **80 and 110 AD**. Yet, we still face these same experiences today.

In my fight to expose the Houston Internal Affairs Division, the precipice that I'm speaking of allowed the following events to occur without anyone being held to account: placing dead bodies from the homicide division in my rental properties; placing drugs in my rental properties; padding my internal affairs files with domestic violence complaints withhold notifying me; destroying medical records used to refute false "erratic behavior" allegations; concealing tainted investigations to avoid lawsuits; conducting illegal surveillance with unauthorized police resources; flagging my payroll with derogatory information, violating record retention statutes; providing other agencies with negative employment references which resulted in my inability to pay my student loan debt, IAD telling tenant, Mickey Barber, to stop paying her lease payment at 17310 Beaver Springs, Houston, Texas which resulted in the property going into foreclosure and a lost of $19, 000.00 dollars in damages; allowing my current residence to be used as leverage by Mr. Suazo, a police officer, working with other officers by transferring his non-payment of association fees to me and then having the HOA association attorney threaten to foreclosure if I didn't pay Mr. Suazo's delinquent HOA fees; showing a private photo of me at home to all employers of a case closed since

1995, IAD telling new employees that the case was still open, and IAD and or Major Offenders contacted my son, Martice Hall, and informed him that he had an outstanding warrant. This false statement resulted in his death due to complications of a life-long kidney ailment.

These acts were conducted under the veil of the law enforcement oath: "I do solemnly swear that I will faithfully execute the duties of a police officer, according to the laws of my jurisdiction, and that I will well and truly serve the community and the city without favor or affection, **malice or ill will**, and that I will to the best of my ability preserve, protect, and defend the Constitution and the laws of this country. So help me God". I would honestly like to say that the aforementioned acts were the work of a few rogue officers who **betrayed their badge. Unfortunately, this was not the case.** The rogue cops played a part but the $ 4 million dollars was allowed by politicians and city leaders. This was the culture of Houston. The 4th largest City in the United States but one that under achieves. During my whole career in law enforcement, I took pride in doing real police work. I was a Houston Park Place Ranger. Our motto: one riot, one ranger. As mentioned, I received nine commendations.

In law enforcement, there is no place for predisposed attitudes and beliefs of racism, age, class, political, or sexual biases. Most officers who participant in the code of silence don't even realize where the code of silence originated from. The "We" versus "Them" mentality is similar to the "Rich Man" in the Lazarus parable. Because of weak leadership, the police code of silence continues to drive a wedge between the police and the communities that they serve. Without an immediate change, political forces will rewrite legislation and Jim Crow will again raise its ugly head. This book signals the need to eliminate the need for a code of silence by leaving the plantation mindset behind. In closing, **Leaving the Plantation Mindset** is not about a time period, a zip code, one's intellect, one's wealth, or one's ethnicity, it about [one's spirituality]. which drives [one's character]. George Orwell claimed that where corruption is common place the truth is a revolutionary idea. Let's hope that's not forever.

All court documents can be downloaded from PACER.

EPILOGUE

This journey is about the double standard of laws, rules, ethics, interest, purpose, truths, intentions, character and spirituality that most Americans face. What is unique here is my demand for accountability and my refusal to wear the clothes of Lazarus. When my former police department alleged that I committed domestic violence and framed me, I couldn't deny it because I was never notified of it. And when I learned of the allegations, I said show me the complaint. Today, thirty years later, I still have not seen the complaint.

As we unpeel the layers of this saga, our first stop is what our beliefs are about affirmative action. The City of Houston for years discriminated against black and brown officers. The remedy consisted of positions allocated to minorities. What the government failed to understand is that you can't expect people's [attitudes] to change by substituting a position in exchange for 400 years of racial hatred and racial entitlement. As a [qualified outsider], I experienced retaliation from racist whites and minorities who felt that the government owed them something. I understood the racist whites but it was the "Uncle

Tom" minorities who conspired with the racist whites to criminally frame me in an attempt to disqualify me from the promotion. I received the position but why did the retaliation continue.

In Smith v. City of Kenper, 428 So. 2d. 1171, 1174 (La. App. 5th Cir.1998), a police officer is responsible for maintaining peace and order, preventing and detecting crime, and enforcing the law. Therefore, the die was cast a long time ago as to the function of the police. How could the police have a conflict of interest in what the law prescribed as to what their duties were. In my particular case, the police were acting in unison with the City of Houston when they approved the scheme to falsely accuse me without notifying me of the charge. The reason for the ratification was based on a lack of integrity. The police department and the City of Houston preferred a candidate who they could count on to accept their **culture of corruption** which included fiscal mismanagement, bogus overtime claims, and using the conspiracy of silence to cover up police and official malfeasance behavior.

Corruption includes an inducement by improper considerations to commit a violation of duty by officials (U,S. v, Brown, 555 F.2d. 407, 415-16, (5th Cir. 1977). Based on this definition, both the City of Houston and the Police were violating their duty of office. Leaving the plantation mindset applies to the [notions] held by many citizens that we should accept "every crime report, every investigative conclusion, and every allegation presented to us by the police officials without critical analysis". Despite evidence of cases highlighted in the Innocent Project across the country, we still find it difficult to believe that the police and public officials would engage in police

EPILOGUE

misconduct or steal money from the public.

In my case, I claimed for thirty years that I was framed by my department and [sought the complaint] to show the racial bias and inaccuracies of the investigation. Instead of the police department, the City of Houston, and the Judge ......**giving me the complaint** or complaints that I was legally entitled to, the City of Houston gave me the May 31, 2018 document which was fabricated to cover up the original fabricated complaint. According to Cole v. Carson, 802 F.3d 752 (5th Cir.2015), the Fifth Circuit ruled that a citizen's due process rights are violated when a police officer deliberately fabricated evidence and uses it to frame a citizen and bring false charges and or accusations against that person. Therefore, based on the law, the evidence is overwhelming that the City of Houston and the Houston Police Department were engaged in a conspiracy to deprive me of my constitutional rights. But why? My answer is the plantation mindset.

Despite harm to my reputation and intentional infliction of emotional distress, the City of Houston and the Police Department's interests were different from mine. Their interest was to suppress the truth and mine was to expose the truth. This clash resulted in more employment retaliation and the continuation of the stigma plus smear campaign resulting in no independent investigations. Therefore, the police department continued to act with impunity since no one at City Hall held them accountable for their misconduct. Leaving the plantation mindset questions whether the police department in my case and others was behaving like a criminal enterprise. In order to answer this question, we have to ask ourselves if the police department has the capacity to break the law, to cover up their misconduct, to use taxpayers monies to finance their illegal overtime schemes, to conceal and to destroy evidence, and do they deny accountability when caught.

In considering the totality of the circumstances known and unknown, I claim that the Houston Police Department and the City of Houston do have the capacity to act like a criminal enterprise when they engage in: a) a conspiracy to suppress the truth, b) when officers engage in police misconduct, c) the mismanagement of financial resources, and d) by falsifying crime reporting. This author claims that in order to understand the role of the police and particularly the internal affairs division, one must redefine the purpose of the internal affairs division. The purpose of the internal affairs division is to suppress the truth and to obstruct justice in order to minimize municipal liability; therefore, their job is to manipulate investigations and to use the code of silence to cover up material and relevant facts. By allowing no outside auditors to inspect or examine police investigations, the results are the Hardy Street drug scandal and 264,000 cases closed without investigations. These are RICO activities which will continue despite the political rhetoric to do better when one does not have **the capacity to be spiritual and ethically endowed to do better**.

Leaving the Plantation Mindset means changing how we examine the crime problem. As a Phd. thinker, I was trained to conceptualize problems in terms of theoretical models. We, in law enforcement, have gathered enough empirical data to know that building a community takes more than "playing basketball or dancing with an inner city youth"; yet, we concentrate on the flaws of the individual rather than the flaws of the system that engulf the individual. In the Movie, V for Vendetta, the protagonist, exposes government officials for fabricating a social crisis so that politicians could come in and rescue the poor.

EPILOGUE

This theme of keeping the poor dependence on politicians for their subsistence replicates itself in our failure to educate our children.... relegating them to the same Plantation Mindset as their parents and grandparents; **then, criticizes them** for their skill and judgment deficiencies. When Albert Einstein stated, "Don't expect the people who caused the problem to solve it", he was not just referring to an individual's training but he was more importantly talking about an individual's impartiality. You can't expect an individual who has an interest in the outcome of a transaction to be fair with all parties. **Conflicts of interest** always influence the outcome of one's behavior. Placing individuals on a task force who will conceal information from the public because their loyalty is to their boss rather than the public is a form of corruption.

Corruption is a form of lying. A person or an institution that lies is a thief because they are robbing you of the truth and the need for transparency. Corruption in the government, policing, courts, corporations, and schools is a form of lying to the public. Corruption must be abated by examining the track record of officials in terms of measurable changes in the [quality of life indexes impacting the public] that those officials have **already achieved and can serve as a litmus test** prior to further consideration for the position that the individual seek. In my situation, the members of City Hall, the Police Department, and the Courts were not concerned with a crime being committed or me being unfit for duty, they were resentful of me using my education and my qualifications as a tool to expose a government characterized by a culture of bribes, financial mismanaged, police brutality, and political corruption. As Frederick Douglass stated, they preferred that I carried myself like a shiftless and ignorant black man who was impervious to the circumstances around me (corruption) and just look the other way. By doing so, I would have satisfied how they wanted me to think and act. Therefore, despite my complaints, the Houston Community affirmed the message, "you stay in trouble because you don't know your place". Therefore, it was this Plantation Mindset that justified their retaliation against me.

In sports, a Jim Brown, Bill Russell, Kareem Abdul Jabbar, Michael Jordan, Larry Bird, Koby, Shaq, Coach Popovich, Ali, Kaepernick, and Magic were leaders on the court and or field who were known as **closers**. Today, we need a new generation of leaders, who understand the implications of spending $8,000 annually to educate a student in comparison to $25,000 to house an inmate in a Texas or Louisiana Correctional Facility. We need leaders who are capable of closing these types of disparities which have plagued us for decades. There is no need for racism in law enforcement, courts, education, business, or sports. In sports, Kyle McNair, the owner of the Texans, made the statement at a golf tournament, "I'm sorry we didn't meet last year because of the China Virus. He was targeting Asians (2021). His dad, the late Bob McNair made a similar comment during the period that Black players took a knee during the National Anthem to protest social injustice and police brutality. The late Bob McNair commented, "We can't have the inmates running the prison". Of course, these were jokes and these gentlemen didn't really mean what they said.

The clarion call for new leaders are not restricted to white men. It includes blacks, browns, and Asians as well. For purposes of clarity , any person can be a niggard or an "Uncle Tom". These names represent characteristics of one's thinking. Webster defines a niggard as a stingy and selfish individual. I define an Uncle Tom as any individual who is content in not wanting any person to grow and to develop as a result of [the judging person's] own insecurities for a need for power and for a need to control other people. For both blacks and whites, leaving the plantation mindset means abandoning any symbiotic relationship based on the superiority v. inferiority model that drives behaviors and relationships because more often than not those relationships are not anchored in the holy spirit. Leaving the plantation mindset means abandoning the **Willie Lynch tactic** where police use race, stereotypes, age, and gender to manipulate people rather than conduct legitimate investigations based on facts. In my case, my ex-wife confessed. Her ex-husband before me, claimed that **she had some mental issues** and he divorced her. The ex-husband worked for the same Houston Police Department. So why didn't IAD contact Holeonal Halliburton. Dr. Joy Leary, in her book, Post Traumatic Slave Syndrome, **traces** the trauma that all black people have suffered as a result of slavery. Today, there is a wealth of research on racial myths and stereotypes so there's [no excuse] for anyone to be **racially illiterate**.

Yet, for 30 years, the Houston Internal Affairs Division and the fourth largest city in the United States, told every employer whom I applied to for employment that I was convicted of domestic violence or that I was mentally unfit for law enforcement. And as a result of the racism and the Uncle Tom nature of these gatekeepers, my reputation continuously smeared. From a constitutional point of view, my only offense was that I demanded the other two fifths of my citizenship according to the laws of this great nation and that my perception of "who I am" was based on who God said "I am". Therefore, my faith does not allow me to wear Lazurus clothing when I can wear my own.

My journey was about an **assignment** which God entrusted me to tell **about a dark place** that God commands the need for change. The story draws a sharp distinction between justice that is based on external man-made laws and societal norms; in contrast to righteousness which embodies God's internal qualities of judgment, wisdom, grace, and mercy. The story reminds us that: "For we wrestle not against flesh and blood, but against principalities, against powers, against the rulers of the darkness of this world, against spiritual wickedness in high places." **Ephesians 6:12.** How do we discern the difference between people's outer appearance of clean and wholesomeness and an inner spirit that can be diabolical, deceptive, manipulative, and evil. In other words, how can one tell who's a "Christian" and who's not? Pastor William J. Barber II, answers this question in a sermon where he first elaborated on Mahatma Gandhiji's seven social sins (1925) : (1) Politics without principles, the absence of an ethical foundation, (2) Wealth without work, accumulation of wealth based on unethical or exploitive means, (3) Pleasure without conscience, personal gratification without caring about the harm or empathy to others, (4) Knowledge without character, the absence of integrity, (5) Commerce without morality, unethical business practices including fraud, deception, and dishonesty, (6) Science without humanity, misuse of scientific discoveries to the detriment of humanity, and (7) Worship without sacrifice, ritualistic worship void of compassion for others. According to Pastor Barber, the manifestation of Gandhiji's seven social sins are the **consequences of when Churches worship god without a conscience.** Pastor Barber explains that individuals can attend church and Pastors can preach every Sunday but be unmoved by social injustices because they have no conscience. Therefore, **they will not be moved** to change social, economic, and political injustices.

EPILOGUE

In my 30 year journey, I spoke to many people about this injustice but no one in the City of Houston and the Courts saw fit to intervene …….only to cover up the injustices. During this whole time, Satan was relentless. Satan chased me every day in an attempt to tempt me to be depressed, to make me feel hopeless, and to try to destroy me with suicidal thoughts. But it was not the people that I prayed to, it was God. And, God responded by sending the Holy Spirit to renew my faith by giving me new wine to pour into new bottles. So in essence, this book represents God's **benediction** to remind others that no matter whatever you are struggling with; God is still on the throne and he will provide what you need. Leaving the Plantation Mindset is about coming into alignment with God's spirit …. not man's.

EVIDENCES

The significance of the evidence section is that before I produced official documents showing that the domestic violence complaint was investigated and dismissed and that the mentally unfit allegations were bogus, the police and the City of Houston officials lied about these facts, distorted the facts, and made up their own facts. The Assistant City Attorney stated that I never provided the police department with medical records; yet, the internal affairs division sergeant stated that I did. When I produced the medical records for court, the internal affairs division had already destroyed the medical records.

These lies by the government continued when I requested my files and the City of Houston provided me with the May 31, 2018 government record which was assessed by a Houston FBI agent as fabricated evidence. However, a Federal Judge allowed the City of Houston to file a false petition in Court and use the fabricated document to dismiss my lawsuit. The Federal Judge, who presided over my initial lawsuit, was the same Judge that presided over the 1994 Affirmative Action lawsuit where the court decree claimed that there would be no discrimination or retaliation against officers who were promoted from the affirmative action lawsuit. This consent decree was violated when the two white lieutenants called me a "welfare lieutenant" which was a racial slur. Yet, my white Captain told me that I was acting erratic because I refused to be insulted and disrespected. When I complained about the racial slur, the white captain told me that I had deep seated emotional problems.

How does one overcome this level of corruption when you give the police and the City of Houston the evidence that they gave you 1995 which exonerated you but on May 31, 2018; they give you a fabricated government record to cover up the first **retaliatory** criminal investigation against you. The significance of this evidence section begs the question as to how **JUSTICE** is [**suppose to look**] when evidence doesn't matter, when you can't cross examine witnesses, when you are not notified of the charges against you, when the Judge won't give you a copy of the investigation, and when the police conduct a diminished investigation, coach witnesses, and threaten process servers. While the evidence shows that these government officials violated my constitutional rights, it also shows throughout this manuscript that the Houston Police Department and the City of Houston has for many years traveled down the slippery slope as a **police state** exercising authoritarian control over the investigative process, charging process, and judicial process …..when Federal Judges ratify police misconduct.

This story sounds the alarm……. that all nations should be concerned when any government acts as a **police state** by curtailing the civil liberties and human rights of its citizens, monitoring their activity, conducting surveillance on its citizens, and then retaliating against them for exercising their discontent. With the advent of AI, facial recognition, drones, media outlets, cell and gps surveillance, these measures of police control will increase as hunger, health, energy, population growth, and poverty increases. Unless we make the government and police more accountable, we will bring the plantation back and all its accouterments. Dr. King reminds us that during periods of injustice, we will not remember the words of our enemies, but we will remember the **silence** of our "friends". Elie Wiesel stated that we may be powerless in terms of preventing injustice but there must never be a time when we fail to protest. I will continue to protest until the unjust become accountable.

AMERICAN INJUSTICE

ORG 10550	ACCT	DESCRIPTION CENTRAL, WS & SE	BUDGET	SPENT	% OVER	NEXT FY REQUEST
FY92	10120	OVERTIME - CIVILIAN	96,600	741,568	668%	(Records Lost)
FY93	10120	OVERTIME - CIVILIAN	359,600	789,474	120%	359,800
FY94	10120	OVERTIME - CIVILIAN	200,000	873,863		200,000
FY95	10121	OVERTIME - CIVILIAN	200,000	N/A		N/A
FY92	10230	OVERTIME - CLASSIFIED	45,000	215,847	380%	(Records Lost)
FY93	10230	OVERTIME - CLASSIFIED	75,000	202,072	169%	75,000
FY94	10230	OVERTIME - CLASSIFIED	75,000	227,813	204%	150,000
FY95	10230	OVERTIME - CLASSIFIED	75,000	N/A		N/A
ORG 10551		DESCRIPTION MUN. DETENTION CENTER				
FY92	10120	OVERTIME - CIVILIAN	20,000	35,226	76%	(Records Lost)
FY93	10120	OVERTIME - CIVILIAN	32,700	54,098	65%	32,700
FY94	10120	OVERTIME - CIVILIAN	23,600	74,781	217%	30,000
FY95	10120	OVERTIME - CIVILIAN	30,000	N/A		N/A

ORG 10550 - CENTRAL, WESTSIDE AND SOUTHEAST
ORG 10551 - MUNICIPAL DETENTION CENTER

*For FY 95 the projected cost of the court mandated 40 hour in-service training for jailers is $365,760

figure 1

4 Million Stolen

EVIDENCES

Academy Class 101

Athlete For Social Justice

Page 13, Investigation Report, Control #94-1

courteous, civil and respectful of their superior officers and associates and shall not use threatening or insulting language."

ADDITIONAL INFORMATION

LAW SUIT PROMOTIONS

There are two lists of promotions made because of law suits. Lieutenant Hall was promoted as a result of the Edward's law suit in which minorities were promoted as a result of purported discrimination against minorities in the testing procedures used by HPD. These promotions have caused some resentment from non-minority officers and supervisors. Another law suit, generally known as the Civilianization law suit, resulted in officers and supervisors being promoted as a result of originally being denied promotions because of a civilianization process during the 1980's which displaced some police supervisory positions with civilians. The appeals courts ruled that this was unfair and ordered the promotion of several officers and supervisors of all ranks.

RELIEF OF DUTY LETTER

Lieutenant Hall was relieved of duty on January 10, 1995, pending an evaluation by the Administrative Personnel Committee. This relief-of-duty status was requested by Lieutenant Hall's supervisors based on their observations of his erratic behavior and correspondence. Attached to this investigation is Lieutenant Hall's relief-of-duty letter which is not related to this investigation.

J. C. Green, Sergeant
Internal Affairs Division

JCG/jcg

Administrative Personnel Administration

Mr. David Liggins, Investigator
Equal Employment Opportunity Commission
Re: John Earl Hall
Page 3

In conjunction with other occurrences, Dr. Leo's evaluation raised legitimate concerns regarding Lieutenant Hall's mental fitness for duty. In fact, once the department received some evidence placing the mental fitness of an officer in question, the department is under a legal duty to investigate. Consequently, pursuant to Loc. Gov't. Code § 143.1115 *Determination of Physical and Mental Fitness* (attachment C), Lieutenant Hall was relieved of duty pending an inquiry into his fitness for duty, and a determination of a suitable environment for his ailment.

At no time did Lieutenant Hall provide opinions from three physicians indicating that he was physically and emotionally able to return to work. Instead, Lieutenant Hall hired a representative who requested an audience with departments official to mediate Lieutenant Hall's concerns. This meeting was attended by four (4) Assistant Chief's of Police, two of which were African-American. During this conference it was Lieutenant Hall's representative who suggested that perhaps the letter was in poor taste and as an offer of settlement, Lieutenant Hall would recant and apologize. The representative stated also that Lieutenant Hall was going through a divorce which contributed to his current high level of anxiety. In return, the representative asked the department to transfer Lieutenant Hall either to the Recruiting, Juvenile, or Criminal Intelligence Division. During the department's consideration of this request, Hall hired another attorney, Ms. Darah Headley.

In correspondence dated February 27, 1995 (attachment D), Ms. Headley stated Lieutenant Hall's position on the matter. In return correspondence dated March 16, 1995 (attachment E), it was explained to Ms. Headley why Hall was relieved of duty and what was required for his return to duty. The department simply asked for a statement from his personal physician that Lieutenant Hall is *capable of performing any duties and of working in any environment without compromise to his mental health.* The department believed that compliance with statute required this comprehensive approach. To date, the statements submitted by Hall only referred to his ability to work his previous assignment. In a letter dated March 21, 1995 (attachment F), Ms. Headley informed the department that she was in the process of securing the appropriate work release and again requested a transfer on behalf of Lieutenant Hall. She subsequently informed the department by telephone that Hall's physician was on maternity leave, the department agreed to accept a statement from her designee.

In correspondence dated March 27, 1995, it was explained to Ms. Headley that the department would not agree to transfer Lieutenant Hall to settle this matter but Hall, like all employees, was free to apply for a voluntary transfer, (attachment G). In a letter dated May 2, 1995 (attachment I), Ms. Headley provided to the department clearing Lieutenant Hall's return to duty. On May 5, 1995, Lieutenant Hall was returned to duty and was assigned to the Southeast Jail, relief position. His referral to the administrative personnel committee was terminated (attachment J).

City Attorney Lies About Medical Records

From
. Lou Reiter
To
. Jay
This wasn't me Jay.
Wed,5:4
On Tuesday, January 15,2013,Jay wrote:
I will forward package to institute address. Awesome.
Sent from my LG phone
Wed, Jan 16,2}13 at 5:45 AM
I
?
Lou Reiter <loureiter@gmail.com> wrote:
>http : //fi orentiniw. altervist
tou Reite. Rotarian since 1976 Co-Director Legal and Liability Risk Management Inst.
associated Public Agency Training Council 706.268.t824 404.242.9069 Cell 887 Chula D
(FedEx, UPS) 10603 Big Canoe Jasper, GA 30143 loureiter@gmail.com

Computer Hacking

EVIDENCES

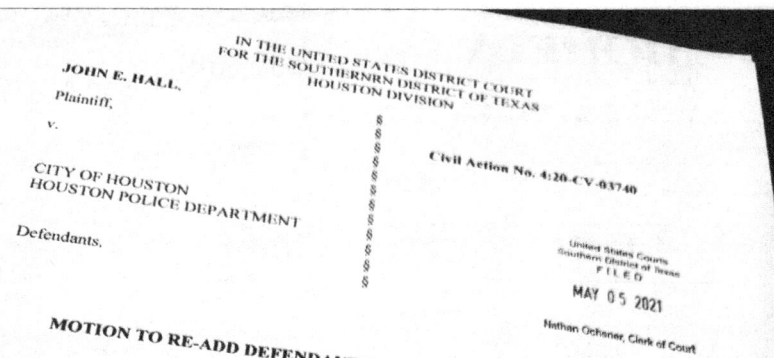

IN THE UNITED STATES DISTRICT COURT
FOR THE SOUTHERNRN DISTRICT OF TEXAS
HOUSTON DIVISION

JOHN E. HALL,
Plaintiff,
v.
CITY OF HOUSTON
HOUSTON POLICE DEPARTMENT
Defendants.

Civil Action No. 4:20-CV-03740

United States Courts
Southern District of Texas
FILED
MAY 05 2021
Nathan Ochsner, Clerk of Court

MOTION TO RE-ADD DEFENDANT MAYOR SYLVESTER TURNER

Plaintiff, John E. Hall, files this motion to re-add Mayor Turner to the lawsuit Under Fed. Rule Civil Procedure 15 (c) based on constructive notice and knowledge of the evidence submitted and contained within the May 31, 2018 document submitted by Defendant, ristie Lewis. At the time of that the evidence was created and submitted to plaintiff, Turner s the Mayor of Houston and Kristie Lewis was an employee of the City of Houston. Further, etter was written as a legitimate government document on City of Houston letter head.

Respectfully,

Dr. John "Jay" Hall

17818 Running Brook Ln.

Spring, Tx. 77379

Obstruction of Justice

```
MOHELA                                              Federal Student Aid
A Department of Education Servicer                  An OFFICE of the U.S. DEPARTMENT of EDUCATION

Find tools and resources to make the best repayment decision for you. Most borrowers can lower their payments by enrolling in the
new SAVE Plan or other income driven plans. Visit StudentAid.gov/restart
  Name                                              Account Number       Date Billed
  JOHN E HALL                                       87 0560 4649         10-30-23        Date Due
                                                                                         11-24-23
  Date Last         Principal Paid Since  Interest Paid Since   Fees Paid Since    Total Pmnts Rcvd
  Payment Received Last Statement        Last Statement        Last Statement     Since Last Statement
                    $0.00                 $0.00                 $0.00              $0.00
  Bill Type         Amount Past Due       Current Due           Total Principal                Outstanding Late
  INSTALL           $2,715.02             $2,715.02             And Interest Due                Fees To Date
                                                                $5,430.04                      $0.00
                                          Monthly
Loan  First   Loan                        Installment  Int
Seq   Disb    Program  Status  Owner      Amount       Rate    Balance      Amount    Current        Total
 1  07/10/14  DLSCNS   REPAY   DEPT OF ED $396.95      5.625%  $36,212.36   Past Due  Amount Due     Amount Due
 2  07/10/14  DLUCNS   REPAY   DEPT OF ED $2,318.07    5.625%  $212,398.51  $396.95   $396.95        $793.90
                                                                            $2,318.07 $2,318.07      $4,636.14
```

Damages

From: Clifford Pope <ssgpope@gmail.com>
To: Jay Hall <jayearl2007@yahoo.com>

Sent: Monday, May 6, 2013 5:28 PM
Subject: Re:

4044058811

Sent from my iPhone

On May 4, 2013, at 10:54 AM, Jay Hall <jayearl2007@yahoo.com> wrote:

Dr. Pope,

Lost phone number. Send number.

Jay

- 1 Attachment
- 4-9-13 Participant S
  .docx
  Download

Dr. Clifford Pope, is currently an ambassador for Capella University. At the time, he presented the audio interview to me, he knew that his interviewing a participant for my study was a violation of IRB guidelines. The question becomes who instructed him to do it.

Retaliation Capella

EVIDENCES

RE: AFFIDAVIT

My name is Gerald F. Mills, I am a retired High School coach and educator from Houston Texas.

I am a military veteran and at one time I had a top security clearance and word in the nuclear missiles program for the United States of America.

I have known Mr. John Jay Hall for thirty-seven years and have fellowshipped with him on a Spiritual and social level during that time. On or about the year 2002, John called me because he needed my assistance at his rental property 3212 Jackson St. Midtown, Houston Tx. Mr. Hall came to my home and we went to said rental property. As we existed the car which was park in front of the complex, I began to smell an odor the like of which I had never smelled in my life. It turned out to be a decaying body, which was located in one of the apartments in Johns' building. I was in total shock because of the smell and the body. John began to pour bleach in the apartment explain to me "it would help eliminate the smell". To this very day, I still tell my friends of that night because it was truly an eye-opening experience.

As I stated in the beginning of this letter, I have known John Hall for thirty-seven years and I am aware of the problems James is having with his son. James is a loving father and an awesome family man. John has always been there for his children and given them all the support, both spiritual and monetary, to make sure they are successful in life. With that being said, John's son has been a disruptive force for quit a while and for what ever reason has turned on his father.

I stand firmly by everything that I have stated in this letter and personally know these things to be true.

Gerald F. Mills

Dead Body Retaliation

Defendant Joaquina Winslow

EVIDENCES

EVIDENTIARY NOTES: (SPECIAL RIGHT OF ACCESS)

October 10, 1997

Mr. Craig Leavers, Investigator, Open Records Division
Office of the State Attorney General
P.O. Box 12548
Austin, Texas 78711-2548

Mr. Leavers:

I am in receipt of your correspondence dated September 19, 1997 in which you stated that this department should have requested an opinion from the Attorney General as to whether or not the Houston Police Department Internal Affairs Division (IAD) file was excepted from inspection and/or copying by Lt. J.E. Hall. This department had taken the position that the fact that IAD files were excepted from public release was settled as a matter of case law (see City of San Antonio v. Texas Attorney General, 851 S.W. 2d 946 [Tex. App. --Austin, 1993, writ denied]) and state statute (see Local Gov't Code §§143.089[g] and 143.1214[b]). It is your opinion that Lt. Hall has a special right of access that may take precedence over the case law and state statutes.

Without waiving any legal argument, the department will make the requested IAD file available to Lt. Hall. However, the department reserves the right to request an opinion on any similar request in the future without the taint of the department being beyond the statutory ten-day limit allowed for requesting an opinion from the Attorney General.

Thank you for your cooperation in this matter and if you have any further questions, please contact the Director of the department's Legal Services Unit, Mr. Craig Ferrell, at (713) 247-5460.

Sincerely,

C.O. Bradford
Chief of Police

Denied Special Right of Access

Mr. David Liggins, Investigator
Equal Employment Opportunity Commission
Re: John Earl Hall
Page 4

After review, the Chief of Police determined that there was insufficient evidence to support the charges levied against Lt. Hall in IAD #94-1649 (attachment K). Lt. Hall was not disciplined, the case was closed.

In conclusion, the Department denies any type of discrimination in violation of federal or state statutes. All employees of the department are afforded equal treatment under State and Federal law and the City of Houston policies. It is the department's belief that these allegations are made solely in an attempt by Lt. Hall to secure a transfer to another assignment.

Sincerely,

Robert G. Lee
Assistant City Attorney

Enclosures

RGL:mg
h:\lee\hall.eeoc

Dismissal Insufficient Evidence

EVIDENCES

David Mitcham
First Assistant/Chief of Courts

Vivian King
First Assistant/Chief of Staff

Harris County District Attorney's Office
1201 Franklin Street, Suite 600
Houston, TX 77002

HARRIS COUNTY DISTRICT ATTORNEY
KIM OGG

November 28, 2023

John Hall

Via email: jayearl2007@yahoo.com

    Re: Public Information Act Request of November 11, 2023
            PIC ID: 2023.11 - 0035

Mr. Hall,

    You recently requested the following from our office:

    [A]ny domestic violence complaints against me at any time.

    A reasonably diligent search of our records has revealed that we possess no information responsive to your request.

    Should you have any questions, I may be reached by phone at 713-274-5816, or by email at scott_meagan@dao.hctx.net.

Sincerely,

Meagan Scott
Assistant General Counsel
Office of the District Attorney
(713) 274-5816

District Attorney Search

AMERICAN INJUSTICE

> Evidence that Exhibit 2 (referenced in my 31, 2018 letter) was fabricated, or does not exist.
>
> If Exhibit #2 has been sealed it is up to the Courts to unseal, and is not a FBI matter
>
> SA Steve Lupo

Evidence FBI Assessment

Ex-wife coached by HPD

EVIDENCES

> Ideas to establish trust in the Marriage:
>
> 8-15-94
>
> Gary has been a good husband and tried to do right things but became frustrated, threw tamptrums and said things that were emotionally damaging because I misinterpreted some of things he said because I was insecure.

Ex-wife Confession

Ex-wife Counseling for Rejection

EVIDENCES

General Ken Paxton   May 31, 2018   2

disciplinary action against a . . . police officer that was overturned on appeal, or any document in the possession of the [police] department that relates to a charge of misconduct against a . . . police officer, regardless of whether the charge is sustained, only in a file created by the [police] department for the [police] department's use. The [police] department may only release information in those investigatory files or documents relating to a charge of misconduct:

    (1) to another law enforcement agency or fire department;

    (2) to the office of a district or United States attorney; or

    (3) in accordance with Subsection (c).

(c) The [police] department head or the [police] department head's designee may forward a document that relates to disciplinary action against a . . . police officer to the director or the director's designee for inclusion in the firefighter's or police officer's personnel file maintained under Sections 143.089(a)-(f) only if:

    (1) disciplinary action was actually taken against the . . . police officer;

    (2) the document shows the disciplinary action taken; and

    (3) the document includes at least a brief summary of the facts on which the disciplinary action was based.

The information contained in **Exhibit 2** consists of an investigation conducted by the HPD's Internal Affairs Division of alleged misconduct by a police officer. Information contained in Exhibit 2 is maintained in the police department's investigatory files and is not part of the police officer's civil service personnel file. The allegations of misconduct were not sustained and no disciplinary action was taken. As such, the information in question does not meet the conditions specified by section 143.1214(c) for inclusion in the police officer's personnel files under section 143.089(a) of the Local Government Code.

Additionally, the requester is not a representative of another law enforcement agency, a fire department, or the office of a district or United States attorney. See id. § 143.1214(b)(1)-(2). Accordingly, the Department believes that it must withhold the information contained in **Exhibit 2** under section 552.101 of the Government Code in conjunction with section 143.1214(b) of the Local Government Code.

Section 552.101 of the Government Code

Section 552.101 of the Government Code excepts from disclosure "information considered to be confidential bylaw, either constitutional, statutory, or by judicial decision." TEX.GOV'T CODE § 552.101. This section encompasses information protected by other statutes. Article 18.20 of the Texas Code of Criminal Procedure pertains to the detection, interception, and use of wire, oral, or electronic

Fabricated Record

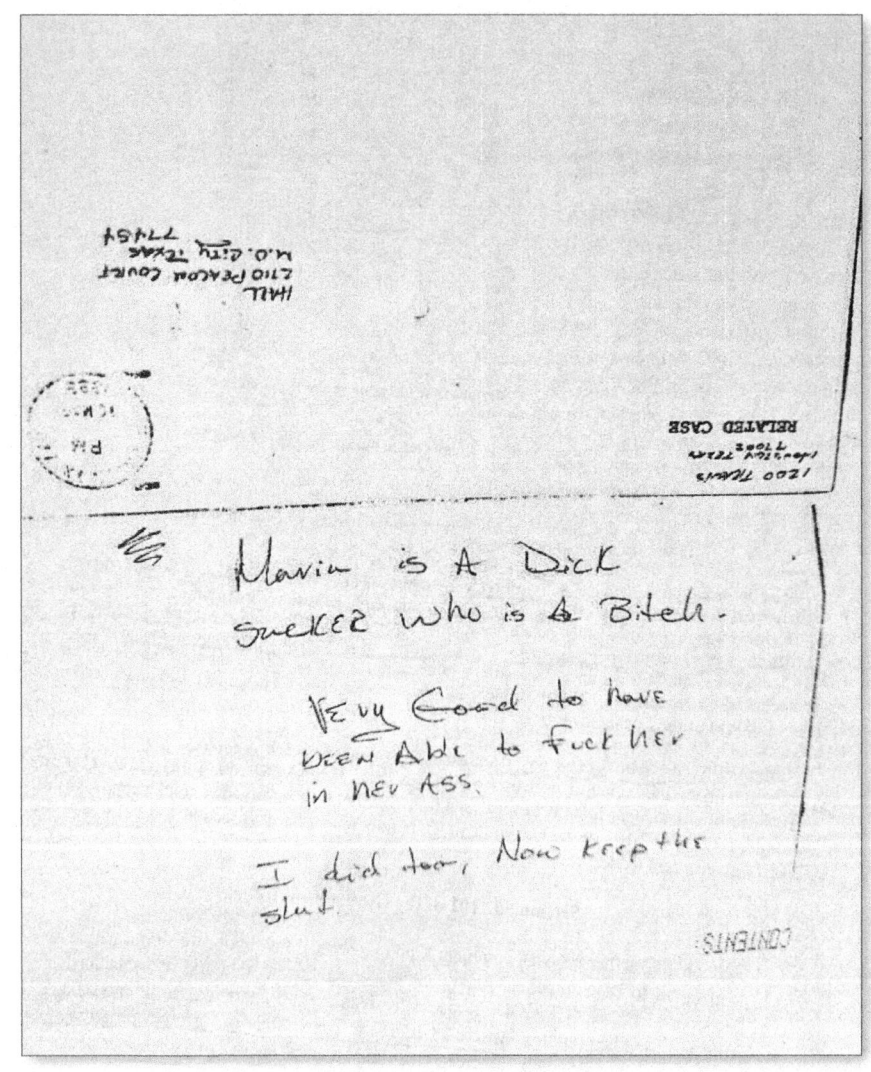

HPD and Ex-wife 1200 Travis

UNITED STATES DISTRICT COURT SOUTHERN DISTRICT OF TEXAS

John E. Hall,
    Plaintiff,

versus

The City of Houston, et al.,
    Defendants.

Civil Action H-20-3740

In Camera Inspection Order

1. By June 11, 2021, the City of Houston must give the court for in camera inspection all complaints related to John E. Hall.

2. By June 11, 2021, the City of Houston must also give the court for in camera inspection the investigation referred to as "Exhibit 2" in the May 31, 2018, letter from Kristie Lewis to the Texas Attorney General.

Signed on May 9, 2021, at Houston, Texas.

Lynn N. Hughes
United States District Judge

In Camera Review

UNITED STATES DISTRICT COURT　　　SOUTHERN DISTRICT OF TEXAS

ENTERED
August 31, 2021
Nathan Ochsner, Clerk

John E. Hall,	§	
	§	
Plaintiff,	§	
	§	
versus	§	Civil Action H-20-3740
	§	
The City of Houston, et al.,	§	
	§	
Defendants.	§	

Order

On August 27, 2021, John E. Hall moved for findings of fact and conclusions of law. He says that this court must prove "that the criminal investigation conducted on Hall was not illegal" and that this court "was not a co-conspirator" in obstructing this judicial process.

As the one who brought this case, Hall – not this Court nor the City of Houston – must show that his claims have merit. This court has reviewed the documents from the City, and they do not support his claims. He is <u>not entitled to these confidential documents</u>, and this court will not give them to him. His motion for findings of fact and conclusions of law "based on omissions, absence of negative findings, spoilage of evidence, and disputed issues" is denied. (90)

Signed on August 31, 2021, at Houston, Texas.

Lynn N. Hughes
United States District Judge

Judge Denied Records

White Camelia
Knights of The Ku Klux Klan

State Office: P.O. Box 684
Cleveland, Texas 77328

November 16, 1996

To Whom It May Concern,

This racially polluted society in which White's find ourselves never ceases to amaze me.

The recent news of a lesser qualified "negro" police officer being promoted to Police Chief is but one more example of the systematic promotion of a less qualifi non-white over more qualified White's which will eventually lead to the destruction of law and order, in Houston, and across this once great land.

Everyone involved in law enforcement can easily identify the majority of the perpetrators of crime in this country.

They, "the criminals", have a distinct, color which makes them easy to identify. "black and brown".

One need only examine the prison population and the riots in St. Petersburg, Florida to verify my statement. With all the filth that Christian Klansmen witness in today's America, such as fagots, race-mixers and their mongrel offspring, anti-christ jews in high places and discrimination and hatred against White's, does it really make sense to put "Buckwheat" in such a position of authority. Putting the fox in charge of guarding the hen house just shows how irresponsible and anti-white the officials of Houston have become.

I've said it before and I'll say it again, the sooner White's leave the city of Houston, the sooner non-white's can wallow in their own filth and destroy what's left of Houston. But this time they wont have anyone but themselves to blame.

Our Heavenly Father Yahweh always demands obedience to His laws which are set forth in the Bible. Nowhere in the Bible is there any mention of tolerance for othe religions or gods, homosexuality or race-mixing.

There is a great number of verses that instruct us to remain separate, "kind after Kind", to reject homosexuality and a firm command "Thou shalt have no other gods before Me".

My point is simply this, our Father in Heaven and Christ our Redeemer guarante a reward for His people that "praise and obey Him". We are also guaranteed punishme for those that do not.

Those in law enforcement, "like yourself", understand that breaking the laws of man makes one a criminal. Likewise the breaking of Gods' law makes one a crimina also.

I know many of you feel as I do. We must work diligently and secretly to insu our future and the future of our people.

ALEA JACTA EST, EXITUS ACTA PROBAT, DOMINUS VOBISCUM

For God, Race and Country.

Charles Lee
Grand Dragon
White Camelia Knights
of the Ku Klux Klan

P.S.

Next time your patrol car is low on fuel be sure to stop at the nearest Texaco

21-20451.622

127

KKK Fyler

David Mitcham
First Assistant/Chief of Courts

Vivian King
First Assistant/Chief of Staff

Harris County District Attorney's Office
1201 Franklin Street, Suite 600
Houston, TX 77002

HARRIS COUNTY DISTRICT ATTORNEY
KIM OGG

November 28, 2023

John Hall

Via email: jaycarl2007@yahoo.com

Re: Public Information Act Request of November 11, 2023
PIC ID: 2023.11 - 0035

Mr. Hall,

You recently requested the following from our office:

[A]ny domestic violence complaints against me at any time.

A reasonably diligent search of our records has revealed that we possess no information responsive to your request.

Should you have any questions, I may be reached by phone at 713-274-5816, or by email at scott_meagan@dao.hctx.net.

Sincerely,

Meagan Scott
Assistant General Counsel
Office of the District Attorney
(713) 274-5816

No Domestic Violence Claims

EVIDENCES

Loren Jackson
HARRIS COUNTY DISTRICT CLERK
P.O. BOX 4651
HOUSTON, TEXAS 77210-4651
Certificate Of Record Search

DATE: 9/24/2009
NAME: HALL, JOHN EARL
DATE OF BIRTH: 1/28/1952
SOCIAL SECURITY NO: 316-58-0034

TO WHOM IT MAY CONCERN:

This certificate is issued under seal, certifying that the information contained herein is a true and correct restatement of the summary, electronic data of the records filed and/or recorded in the District Clerk's Office, as it appears on this date.

The search results are dependent on identifiers entered by the user.

A criminal record search was conducted from 1976 to the present and no criminal charges were found on the above individual. This criminal record search was conducted using the individual's name, date of birth, and/or Social Security number. No federal or other County's records, or Justice of the Peace or other Municipalites Class C Misdemanors will be Displayed.

This certificate is issued only as to a search conducted for records on file with the District Clerk of Harris County, Texas.

This record search does not include names of defendants, indicted directly by the grand jury, unless the defendant is in custody or under bond, pursuant to Vernon's Texas Ann. C.C.P. Article 20.22.

Loren Jackson
District Clerk Harris County, Texas

201 CAROLINE ~ PO BOX 4651 ~ HOUSTON, TEXAS 77210-4651 ~ (713) 755-7300

No Criminal Record

Mr. David Liggins, Investigator
Equal Employment Opportunity Commission
Re: John Earl Hall
Page 3

In conjunction with other occurrences, Dr. Lee's evaluation raised legitimate concerns regarding Lieutenant Hall's mental fitness for duty. In fact, once the department received some evidence placing the mental fitness of an officer in question, the department is under a legal duty to investigate. Consequently, pursuant to Loc. Gov't. Code § 143.1115 *Determination of Physical and Mental Fitness* (attachment C), Lieutenant Hall was relieved of duty pending an inquiry into his fitness for duty, and a determination of a suitable environment for his ailment.

At no time did Lieutenant Hall provide opinions from three physicians indicating that he was physically and emotionally able to return to work. Instead, Lieutenant Hall hired a representative who requested an audience with departments official to mediate Lieutenant Hall's concerns. This meeting was attended by four (4) Assistant Chief's of Police, two of which were African-American. During this conference it was Lieutenant Hall's representative who suggested that perhaps the letter was in poor taste and as an offer of settlement, Lieutenant Hall would recant and apologize. The representative stated also that Lieutenant Hall was going through a divorce which contributed to his current high level of anxiety. In return, the representative asked the department to transfer Lieutenant Hall either to the Recruiting, Juvenile, or Criminal Intelligence Division. During the department's consideration of this request, Hall hired another attorney, Ms. Darah Headley.

In correspondence dated February 27, 1995 (attachment D), Ms. Headley stated Lieutenant Hall's position on the matter. In return correspondence dated March 16, 1995 (attachment E), it was explained to Ms. Headley why Hall was relieved of duty and what was required for his return to duty. The department simply asked for a statement from his personal physician that Lieutenant Hall *is capable of performing any duties and of working in any environment without compromise to his mental health.* The department believed that compliance with statute required this comprehensive approach. To date, the statements submitted by Hall only referred to his ability to work his previous

No Medical Report

BACON PSYCHIATRIC ASSOCIATES

Robert J. Bacon, Jr.
M.D.

1315 Calhoun • Suite 1200 • Houston, Texas 77002

(713) 655-9410

January 17, 1995

RE: John E. Hall

TO WHOM IT MAY CONCERN;

I examined Mr. John Hall on January 17, 1995 and found that: 1) he exhibits no evidence of mental or emotional pathology or instability and 2) he does in fact appear to be quite healthy mentally, very mature and of sound mind and judgement.

Respectfully,

Robert J. Bacon, Jr., M.D.
RJB/tah

Original received by J. Earl Hall

Medical Report

MEDICAL CORRESPONDENCE

Attached to this investigation are three letters that Lieutenant Hall faxed to the Internal Affairs Division that have no bearing on this investigation. The letters, addressed to Captain Barber, are from medical doctors regarding Lieutenant Hall's mental health.

SECTION 3.1 OF THE RULES MANUAL

Attached to this investigation is a copy of the Rules Manual, section 3.1, Respect for Fellow Employees. "Officers shall treat other members of the department with respect. They shall be

Page 13, Investigation Report, Control #94-1\

courteous, civil and respectful of their superior officers and associates and shall not use threatening or insulting language."

ADDITIONAL INFORMATION

LAW SUIT PROMOTIONS

There are two lists of promotions made because of law suits. Lieutenant Hall was promoted as a result of the Edward's law suit in which minorities were promoted as a result of purported discrimination against minorities in the testing procedures used by HPD. These promotions have caused some resentment from non-minority officers and supervisors. Another law suit, generally known as the Civilianization law suit, resulted in officers and supervisors being promoted as a result of originally being denied promotions because of a civilianization process during the 1980's which displaced some police supervisory positions with civilians. The appeals courts ruled that this was unfair and ordered the promotion of several officers and supervisors of all ranks.

RELIEF OF DUTY LETTER

Lieutenant Hall was relieved of duty on January 10, 1995, pending an evaluation by the Administrative Personnel Committee. This relief-of-duty status was requested by Lieutenant Hall's supervisors based on their observations of his erratic behavior and correspondence. Attached to this investigation is Lieutenant Hall's relief-of-duty letter which is not related to this investigation.

J. C. Green, Sergeant
Internal Affairs Division

Contradiction Medicare Report 3

EVIDENCES

CITY OF HOUSTON
INTER OFFICE CORRESPONDENCE

TO: John Hall
Police Officer
Employee #77253

FROM: Sam Nuchia
Chief of Police

DATE: May 5, 1995

SUBJECT: Return to Duty

The internal investigation into allegations of misconduct by you has been concluded and the Chief of Police has determined the appropriate disciplinary action to be taken in this case. You will be officially notified of discipline to be taken in this matter at a later date.

In light of the completion of this investigation, you will resume your official duties with the Houston Police Department on May 5, 1995.

You are to deliver this letter to the Police Personnel Division where your official identification, badge, hat shield, and building identification will be returned to you. Upon receiving your identification and other equipment from the Personnel Division, you will contact your Division Commander in order to be returned to duty.

Sam Nuchia
Chief of Police

Received by:

_____
John Hall

BY: _____
D. W. Curry, Lieutenant
Internal Affairs Division

DWC:vja
C\ROD.rtdjh

No Mental Help Issue

> **EVIDENTIARY LOG:**
>
> The above conspiracy to conceal background information about police chief candidates has been a practice within the Houston Police Department for some time. Prior to the oral sex incident associated with Chief Acevedo, the police vetting process failed to disqualify another Houston Police Chief. Below is a synopsis of that particular case. **Where's the Me, Too movement in Houston?**
>
> **Chief Charles McClelland (2008)**
>
> Former Police Lieutenant Shannon Broze was forced to resign due to a collateral damage investigation directed by Assistant Chief McClelland after their sexual relationship was detected by her boyfriend. In fact, the Chief was alleged to have been caught having **oral sex in his office**. Once the boyfriend decided to go public with the situation, Assistant Chief McClelland used the fact that Broze confided in him that she had purchased her boyfriend, an ex-con, an assault rifle. Chief Clelland used this revelation as leverage over Lt. Broze and had IAD conduct an investigation. Lieutenant Broze was forced to resign. The gun case is a violation of U.S. Code 18, section 922. Assistant Chief McClelland did not refer the matter to ATF for prosecution,

Oral Sex Part 1

> because an outside investigation would disclose how he obtain the information from former Lieutenant Shannon Broze and would show his complicity in having oral sex on duty with a subordinate. The case can be verified by Broze gun purchase application for the assault rifle. If one were to grant her prosecutorial immunity, her testimony would begin to unwind the tapestry of corruption that was become the norm with respect to how the internal affairs unit conducts its investigations.
>
> In this case alone, federal laws were violated, yet ignored because Assistant Chief McClelland had used the false report prepared by Internal Affairs to gain leverage and to force former Lieutenant Broze to resign. Her silence allows her to find another job without fear of the internal affairs unit disseminating the false report to other law enforcement agencies. In another incident and despite a background check, Assistant Chief McClelland was cleared by an independent search firm authorized by Annise Parker when the search firm failed to disclose that Lieutenant McClelland and wife, Tammie McClelland, engaged in a **firearm shoot out** at their residence in Missouri City, Texas. This incident did not keep McCelland from becoming Chief.
>
> **Chief Hubert Acevedo (2016)**
>
> On May 30, 2008, Chief Hubert Acevedo ("Acevedo") terminated APD Sergeant Dustin Lee and issued a memorandum explaining that Lee had been terminated for sexual harassment and dishonesty. Three days later, Officer Smith was serving as a patrol officer on the evening shift when he overheard several other officers discussing Lee's termination.

Oral Sex Part 2

IN 2014, THE AUSTIN COMMUNITY GROUP REFERRED TO AS PEACEFUL STREETS WERE PROTESTING THE BACKGROUND OF CHIEF ACEVEDO.

Peaceful Streets Project
October 30, 2014

Update on CHP nude photos case: Details of text messages between officer discussing explicit photos stolen from victim's phone. This has been going on for years at CHP even current Austin Police Department chief Art Acevedo participated in this activity when he was employed at CHP. The difference is Acevedo used Polaroids of his victims and carried them around in his glove box to show his pig buddies. Acevedo was sued for $5M. The harassment claims say the woman is a 36-year-old officer from Southern California who had a six- or seven-month affair with Acevedo. She says she posed for the photographs at Acevedo's suggestion, but didn't learn they had been shown to anyone until she was approached by two CHP internal affairs investigators March 17.

The woman, a 13-year department veteran, says in one claim that she was "absolutely horrified and humiliated" when she found out. "I feel that my reputation has been irreparably tarnished, and my career as a CHP officer is essentially over."

Two CHP captains allegedly have said Acevedo showed them the pictures, including one in which the woman is **performing a sexual act on him.**

The woman, who has since married another CHP officer and has two children, says she cannot return to work because rumors and the potential damage to Acevedo's promotion have created a sexually hostile work environment. She has been granted a state disability claim on the grounds that she suffered a stress injury because she was victimized in "a high-profile sexual harassment investigation."

NOTE: ME TOO, MOVEMENT? POLICE INTERNAL AFFAIRS DIVISION
[SIZE=2]Then on July 9th, news hit that CHP Assistant Chief Art Acevedo, a prominent candidate to replace Helmick, was in trouble. According to the Press Democrat, Acevedo "has been the subject of a recent state sexual harassment investigation and a $5 million civil claim for allegedly showing nude photographs of a subordinate officer to high-ranking officials while on duty . . . Acevedo kept sexually explicit photographs of the woman in the glove compartment of his state-issued ca and displayed them to various supervisors between 1995 – when his brief affair with the officer ended – and 2002, according to claims filed with three state agencies . . ."[/SIZE]
[SIZE=2]When he took the photos, Acevedo was a sergeant – guess where! – in the agency's internal affairs bureau! At the time the lawsuit was filed, the CHP had taken no disciplinary acti against Acevedo.[/SIZE]

Oral Sex Part 3

Record Number	Record Title	Record Description	Retention Period
*PS4075-01c	INTERNAL AFFAIRS INVESTIGATION RECORDS	Records of investigations that find an officer engaged in misconduct and penalize the officer below the level of a written reprimand, or of investigations whose findings are inconclusive.	5 years, provided a 1 year infraction-free period precedes the date of destruction.
*PS4075-01d	INTERNAL AFFAIRS INVESTIGATION RECORDS	Records of investigations whose allegations are not sustained, or in cases where accusations are determined to be unfounded or the accused is exonerated.	3 years.
PS4075-01e	INTERNAL AFFAIRS INVESTIGATION RECORDS	Written complaints and records of oral complaints received from the public concerning the conduct of law enforcement officers, fire department personnel, and emergency medical personnel that do not lead to an internal affairs investigation.	Determination not to initiate an internal affairs investigation + 2 years.

Record Retention Violation

EVIDENCES

FROM: Carlton E. Brown   HPD Employee #078774
        11971 White Oak Landing
        Conroe, Texas 77385

To Whom it May Concern

It is my sincerely stated recollection that I had several conversations with acquaintances/friends/colleagues where the subject of Lieutenant John Hall was raised.

These conversations took place in the mid to late 1990s (over 20 years ago) and I do not recall all that was said or even who the conversations were with. I do not believe that the main subject of such conversations were and I doubt that Hall was the main topic of discussion. Such conversations took the form of gossip/rumors/the "grapevine"/scuttlebutt and were highly informal talks between individuals.

On a number of such occasions, Lieutenant Hall's name came up and it was always in the form of insulting insinuations regarding his mental stability and fitness for command.

At this time, I had known Lieutenant Hall for about 10 years or more and considered him a friend and colleague. Though I had not worked directly with Hall for some time I had spoken with him a few times at some length. I found these insinuations to be completely at odds with the John Hall that I knew.

I have NEVER known Lieutenant Hall to be irrational or even remotely mentally unstable and I personally considered him to be totally fit for positions of command and high responsibility.

I would like to add that I have had occasion to obtain "PEN Registers" for investigative purposes during my tenure as an Auto Theft Detective. It is my recollection that such investigative tools ALWAYS required a Court Order to obtain.

signature
5-12-21

21-20451,824

Stigma Plus

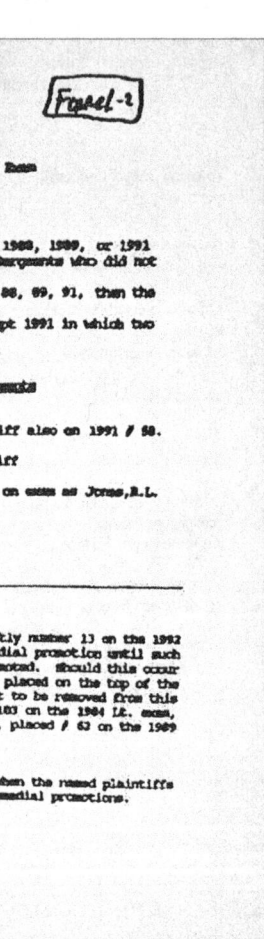

Sergeant Coach Ex-wife

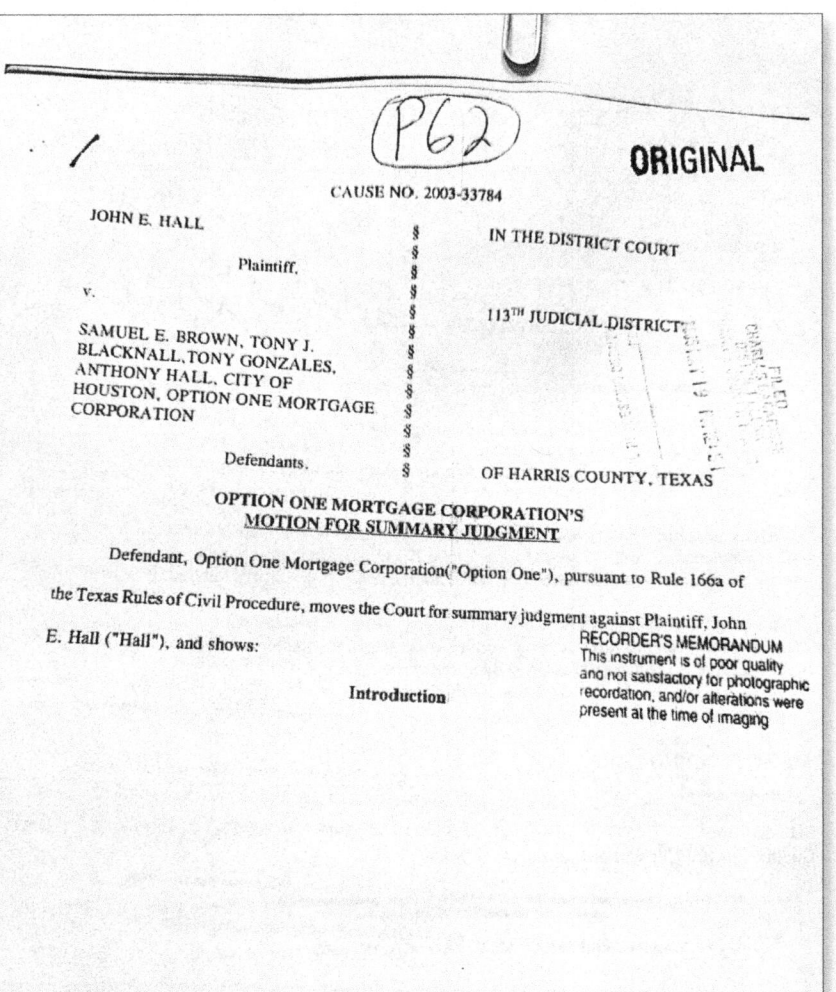

Tony Black HPD CI

CONFIDENTIAL

Impac Funding Corporation

Tuesday, December 03, 2002

HALL PROPERTY MANAGEMENT
2710 PECAN COURT
MISSOURI CITY, TX, 77459

Borrower Name: KARINA SEGOVIA
IFC Loan Number: 1100354176

713- 457-0281
Lead Connection
12-16-04
4-32 pm

To whom it may concern,

As part of Impac Funding Corporation's ongoing Underwriting Compliance Program, we are conducting a random audit of our residential mortgage loans to maintain quality lending standards and to ensure the accuracy of the information submitted.

We have attached a photocopy of the original VERIFICATION OF RENT that was completed by you. We would appreciate it if you would take the time to re-verify the accuracy of the information and mark the respective spaces attached.

Thank you for your time and consideration in this matter. A postage paid envelope has been provided for your convenience. If you should have any questions, please contact me at (949) 475-3600.

Cordially,

IMPAC FUNDING CORP.

Shauna Lopez
Quality Control Department

The confidentiality of the information you have furnished will be preserved except when disclosure of this information is required by applicable law.

1401 Dove Street, Newport Beach, CA. 92660 Telephone(949)475-3600 Fax(949)475-3670

Tony Blacknall FBI Case

The following section describes the transcript of the meeting by Michelle Erickson. On January 3, 1996, Captain One, Captain Two, and myself attended the meeting. As per the transcript, Captain One stated: "The letter concerned me, and it concerned me because I feel that it demonstrates perhaps a deep-seated emotional problem that I certainly can't address. You... Lieutenant Hall: On whose part? Captain One: On your part. And we'll get to that a minute. You know the situation as it was when I came up here. I had a meeting with the assistant chiefs about some of the things you had been involved in. You have a meeting and we never really sat down and shared those things; but as a result of my promotion here, hopefully you can look back and you can reflect to see you and I have spent a lot of time together. I've had you in here with other people off of your shift and we've tried to work out problems in a collegial atmosphere and I've felt that we made considerable progress. Because I really thought we'd made progress, the letter came as a shock. The bottom line to this is I've taken that letter and I've put a cover letter on it and I've sent it up the chain of command and I'm asking that the APC look

at it and review it and then deal with it based on their findings. If I'm going to make that kind of recommendation, I feel that we need to change your assignment temporarily. This may take six to eight weeks. In the meantime, you are assigned to my office from 8am. To 4pm, Monday thru Friday. You will have no supervisory responsibility for your shift. They, in fact, will be aware of it. I do not want another letter from you that questions my authority and my decisions making in regards to this shift. And the Chief of Police wants you to know that any activity on your part otherwise will be deemed insubordination. On the next page is a copy of the Captain's letter.

White Captain False Statements

February 2, 2011

John E. Hall
17310 Beaver Springs Drive
Houston, TX 77090

Dear Mr. Hall:

In response to your letter dated January 7, 2011, Amrent, Inc., has received your dispute and has completed its investigation of your dispute. Enclosed is a revised consumer credit report showing any corrections or updates. The results of the investigation are as follows:

Criminal Record Battery Domestic Violence – Removed
Public Record: Eviction -Wells Fargo Bank N.A. Trustee Fo vs. John E. Hall, Case No. EV61C0012318 – Confirmed

We verified the eviction public record by contacting the Harris County Justice of the Peace 6, Place 1 (713) 921-1576, and reviewing the case information.

You are entitled to add a statement disputing the accuracy or completeness of the information. Please review the attached documents for additional rights under state and federal law.

Sincerely,

AmRent, Inc.
Consumer Relations Department
1-888-898-6196

AmRent Letter

Mr. David Liggins, Investigator
Equal Employment Opportunity Commission

    Re:
    John
    Earl
    Hall
Page 4

After review, the Chief of Police determined that there was insufficient evidence to support the charges levied against Lt. Hall in IAD #94-1649 (attachment K). Lt. Hall was not disciplined, the case was closed.

In conclusion, the Department denies any type of discrimination in violation of federal or state statutes. All employees of the department are afforded equal treatment under State and Federal law and the City of Houston policies.

It is the department's belief that these allegations are made solely in an attempt by Lt. Hall to secure a transfer to another assignment.

                        Sincerely,

                        Robert G. Lee
                        Assistant City
                        Attorney

                        Enclosures

RGL:Eng
klechd

Insufficient Evidence

December 19, 2022

Alamdar S. Hamdani,

United States Attorney

Well Fargo Plaza

1000 Louisiana St. #2300

Houston, Texas 77002

Re: Public Corruption, Judicial Misconduct, Possible Bribery, Political Favors, Civil Rights Violations and Obstruction of Justice Complaint

Congratulations on your recent appointment. My name is John E. Hall, I have two masters degrees and a doctorate in organization behavior, management, and leadership which I achieved on my own with no political favors. I came to Houston to join the Houston Police Department in 1981. In 1994, the City of Houston was in the process of settling an affirmative action lawsuit. Judge Lynn Hughes presided over this case. Due to my test scores, I was placed on both the affirmative action promotional list and the regular promotional test list. Due to politics, the affirmative action promotional list was being manipulated. This fact was known by the defendants listed in my federal lawsuit under 4:20 -CV- 03740 and my appeal under No. 21-20451. As a result of exposing this corruption, the Houston Police Internal Affairs division placed "reputation damaging complaints" in my internal affairs record without notifying me; thereby, stigmatizing my reputation for 28 years in order to prevent me from gaining future employment in law enforcement and paying my federal student loan debt.

From 1994 to May 31, 2018, the Houston Police Internal Affairs Division never informed me that a criminal investigation was conducted and that they placed the criminal complaint in my internal affairs file which was based on a citizen's complaint, where the (ex-wife) was conspiring with an officer who could not pass the promotional exam but who was politically connected; and who felt that she was entitled to the affirmative action promotion). Judge Hughes was aware via transcripts that there was manipulation of the promotional list occurring but

Letter to U.S. Attorney Alamdar Hamdani

Made in the USA
Coppell, TX
29 April 2024

31849001R00066